The Complete K-5 WRITING WORKSHOP

Connecting Process, Writing Skills, and Management

Susan Koehler

The Complete K-5 Writing Workshop
Connecting Process, Writing Skills, and Management

By Susan Koehler

Cover and book design: Mickey Cuthbertson

Library of Congress Cataloging-in-Publication Data

Koehler, Susan, 1963-
The complete K-5 writing workshop : connecting process, writing skills, and management / Susan Koehler.
p. cm.
Includes bibliographical references.
ISBN 978-1-936700-43-1 (pbk.)
1. English language--Composition and exercises--Study and teaching (Elementary) I. Title.
LB1576.K562 2011
372.62'3044--dc23
2011028627

Maupin House publishes professional resources for K-12 educators. Contact us for tailored, in-school training or to schedule an author for a workshop or conference. Visit www.maupinhouse.com for free lesson plan downloads.

Maupin House Publishing, Inc. by Capstone Professional
1710 Roe Crest Drive
North Mankato, MN 56003
www.maupinhouse.com
800-524-0634
352-373-5588
352-373-5546 (fax)
info@maupinhouse.com

Printed in the United States of America in Eau Claire, Wisconsin.
102014 008583R

Dedication

For the children who continually teach me...

Table of Contents

Acknowledgments

Although the words didn't begin appearing on paper until just a few years ago, the writing of this book has been a process spanning many, many years. Since 1985, I have had the privilege of fulfilling a childhood dream: I have been a teacher. My life has been shaped, blessed, enriched, and nourished by the genuine love and potent inspiration of so many children.

When I began to search for samples of children's work to display various craft skills and stages of writing development in this book, I first went to my garage, remembering a wicker basket I had stored away, just in case I ever wrote a book about teaching children to write. I recalled that I had squirreled away the early scribbles of my own children, not only because they were sentimental artifacts, but also because they were ripe examples of various stages of writing development—just in case I ever wrote a book.

Next, I dug through the overloaded top drawer of my filing cabinet. There was a packed file labeled "Writing." Behind it, there was another file labeled "Writing" because I couldn't fit any more paper in the first folder. Behind it, there was another.... Through the years, I had tucked away samples of student work—pieces that brought back sweet memories, pieces that made me laugh, pieces that filled my heart with pride, and pieces that would be great to use—just in case I ever wrote a book.

Well, the book is finally written. In it, you will find many examples of children's writing. Every one of them is special, and for every one that is included, there are a hundred others stuffed in a file or seared in my memory. What greater gift is there than to be a part of the creative process with young minds, watching the light in a child's eyes when an idea materializes or the pride on a child's face when the words on the page come together to convey a thought or feeling?

I have taught children at every grade level between kindergarten and fifth grade. I have enjoyed the privilege of being present when they first began to connect letters to sounds and form written words; I've known the thrill of seeing them string words into sentences and sentences into paragraphs; I have watched as they created characters, supported opinions, and found just the right words to describe a beautiful scene or a heartfelt emotion.

Many of the samples of children's writing appearing in this book were written in recent years. Many others were written years ago by children who have now become adults. Joseph's kindergarten work appears in this book; Joseph is now serving abroad in the U.S. Army. Dean wrote his poem in second grade; he's now in college. Ryan's piece was written when he was in first grade; he is currently a college graduate contemplating law school.

For every writing sample, there is a student; for every student there is a story; each of their stories has become a part of my story. Every child I have taught has helped to shape me—as a person, as a teacher, and as a writer. And so, I wish to acknowledge them all with gratitude and affection—those whose work appears in this book and those whose work remains etched in my memory and in my heart. To all of my students and to my own beautiful children: *thank you*.

Introduction

"It is the supreme art of the teacher to awaken joy in creative expression and knowledge."

—Albert Einstein

I hate writing. If you're a writing teacher, these are the most dreaded words to hear from your students. You picture enthusiasm, excitement, creativity, possibilities...and you find yourself with students who want to finish the assignment as quickly as possible and move on to something more enjoyable.

I clearly remember standing in front of a class of fourth graders and hearing those words. *We hate writing.* It was the general consensus of the class. Discouragement weighed down on me as I faced a year of teaching writing, complete with quarterly district writing tests and a fourth-grade state assessment. So I sat down and asked them *why.*

Overwhelmingly, my students told me that they never got to write what they wanted to write. They were always given topics and prompts. They were told *what* to write and *how* to write it. They were given time limitations and paragraph requirements.

Ah, enlightenment. They didn't hate writing; they hated the way writing was being taught. These students were creative beings, wanting to have some freedom and ownership over the writing process. I'm so glad that I sat down and asked *why.*

So then I asked, *What can I do to make writing more enjoyable?* I was responsible for the state standards, and I would have to prepare them for district and state assessments. Therefore, we would have to do some prompted, timed writing. However, we worked out a compromise that hinged on what we called "free writing."

I went to a local discount store and purchased very inexpensive spiral notebooks for all of my students. These became our "free-writing journals." I guaranteed my students that I would give them at least ten minutes of free-writing time each day. The deal was on.

My journal rules were simple: *You may write whatever you like, as long as it is school appropriate (no graphic violence, offensive language, etc.) and as long as there is no derogatory language aimed at another student. Choose your own mode, genre, topic, and length.* Of course, the other rule was that during that free-writing time, *you must write.*

What my students realized is that they had a lot to say. Those journals became sacred. Some children wrote poetry, and others wrote stories. Some wrote informational pieces, and a couple of students wrote plays. Several children kept a personal journal for recording experiences and exorcising negative emotions.

Most importantly, they realized that they actually *liked* writing. That free-writing time was so important to them that when fire drills, assemblies, or other interruptions pre-empted our usual plans, they still held me to the minimum of ten minutes per day of free-writing time. Several times, they asked if we could skip recess so that they could *write*!

I learned something as well. In the age of accountability, so much of our classroom practice became shaped by testing. It wasn't a matter of "teaching the test." Instead, it was a move away from *process*-oriented to *product*-oriented instruction.

We created time limits and numerical scores to apply to every subject. We set isolated, skills-based goals and standards, and when students met them, we raised the bar. It sounded good. It sounded effective. The numbers were going up. In reality, however, we created young people who wanted to finish the product and move on.

They could answer multiple-choice questions, read a passage in one minute, and write a five-paragraph essay in forty-five minutes. But they missed the integration and generalization that are so important to developing critical thinkers who see the connections between disciplines and build a big picture. And sadly, to a large extent, we lost learner engagement.

In writing, that loss of engagement translated into students who failed to invest themselves in the creative process. Being safe trumped taking risks, so writing started to look formulaic and contrived. Genres were reduced to narrative and expository modes of writing that looked uniform in length and style.

I became reflective, remembering a time when my students loved writing. What was different? It wasn't a search into distant history. I only had to revisit Donald Graves, Lucy Calkins, and even more recently, Marcia Freeman, to remember that writing is a process, and that process precedes the product.

I began to make decisions and shift my focus back to a writers' workshop approach. I still covered the standards. I prepared my students for district and state assessments, but those instruments did not form the centerpiece of my curriculum.

We dissected literature models to discover what seemed to be important to writers, and we built those discoveries into our writing. Students searched their own histories, feelings, opinions, and interests to determine what material was lying dormant within them, waiting to be written.

Through the study and practice of literature models and literary devices, self-selected topics and formats, and a focus on *quality* and *process*, I rediscovered joy in teaching. My students made personal investments and developed pride and ownership in their writing.

However, in unleashing this motivation and passion for writing, I never sacrificed explicit writing-craft instruction. I learned to plan and implement systematic skill instruction, monitor student progress, provide intervention as needed, and still maintain a process-oriented writing workshop where children felt empowered to be creative thinkers and writers.

As teachers, we continually watch the pendulum of pedagogy swing. At one extreme, we have rigid standards, isolated skill instruction, and perpetual numerical measures of achievement. At the other, we have a holistic, student-centered hodge-podge of generalizations without clear, systematic objectives.

In education, as in life, *balance* is the safest and sanest approach. We must resist the urge to be drawn to one extreme or the other. Instead, we must constantly strive to do what is meaningful and effective for our students. In other words, we must use our informed professional judgment and *do what makes sense.*

How to Use This Book

This book is written as a resource for teachers who want to take charge of their own writing curriculum and join the best practices from each extreme to create a rich learning environment. Start by reading about the history of writing instruction (**Chapter 1**), the writing process, and assessment (**Chapter 2**). Then learn what to *do* with detailed information on creating a successful writing workshop (**Chapter 3**)—including writer's and teacher's notebooks, management tips, and publishing projects—and what to *teach* with a list of writing-craft skills and genre instruction guidelines (**Chapter 4**) that form the content of writing instruction. An extensive **Appendix** provides rubrics, checklists, planners, graphic organizers, practice sheets, activities, and more to use in your classrooms today.

By uniting process and skills, we can maintain a systematic approach to instruction while reviving learner engagement and rediscovering the joy of teaching writing.

Chapter One
A Brief History of Writing Instruction

"Arriving at one goal is the starting point to another."

—John Dewey

For years we have listened to the persuasive voices of educational researchers and sales consultants. *There is a new approach. What we have done in the past was misguided and ineffective. Now we know how to ensure achievement for all students!* Teachers who had effectively taught children for years began to doubt their methods; and with the gusty winds of change, they willingly threw the proverbial baby out with the bath water.

Why is it when a new idea comes along in education, we rush to discredit our former practice? We try to teach our students to be critical thinkers as we too easily abandon critical thinking. Every day we make dozens of instructional decisions. We witness the *ah-ha* of discovery and quickly strategize when we see confusion wash across the faces of our students.

Being steeped in daily practice, we know how to use the foundation of our experience to discern *what works* from *what doesn't work*. As with most disciplines, the teaching of writing has encountered abrupt shifts in practice during the course of its evolution. But as reflective practitioners, we should be able to assimilate new methods and strategies into what we already know to be sound practice.

In this book, we will build consensus. We will explore ways to take the best of explicit skill instruction and merge it with the writing process. We will find ways to ensure that our students are achieving writing standards while applying their skills in a meaningful, authentic context.

When we allow ourselves to think critically and make professional choices, we will empower ourselves to choose best practices in the teaching of writing, regardless of methods, movements, and buzz words. In this context, our writing instruction will ensure achievement *and* produce learner engagement. And as teachers, we will rediscover the joy of teaching writing.

A Professional Journey

Once upon a time, when writing was taught as a component of language arts, teachers periodically assigned story starters and students developed creative responses. I will always remember my wonderful, language-loving fifth-grade teacher, Mrs. Smith, asking us to complete a piece that began: *If I had a pair of magic shoes....*

Being a language-loving student, I enjoyed Mrs. Smith's periodic story-starter assignments. My pieces were usually shared with the class and posted on the bulletin board. I received positive reinforcement and continued to write. Writing came naturally to me and I was enthusiastic about it. However, I was not given writing instruction. Mrs. Smith made the assumption that I could write.

(For other students, I can only imagine the anxiety and displeasure those story starters generated. Staring at a blank page and being expected to fill it with a completely new creation can be frightening, especially without instructional support!)

When I became a teacher, my enthusiasm for writing continued. I assigned story starters, but realized that only a small percentage of students could produce a substantive response. I decided that my students did not write often enough and that, with more practice, they would become better writers.

My plan of daily writing practice was not unique. At the time, journaling was gaining popularity, and designating a daily writing time as part of the instructional day was common practice. My students' writing improved due to frequency, attention to their written pieces, and the peer modeling that occurred as they shared their pieces with each other. However, there was still no formal writing instruction taking place.

And then I read Donald Graves' landmark book, *Writing: Teachers and Children at Work* (Heinemann, 1983), and I learned about the writing process. I began to instruct my students in the steps writers take to build a piece of writing. I assured them that they had a wealth of experience and vocabulary to use in writing. They generated personal idea banks and created plans for each piece they began to write. Continuously, their writing evolved through stages: pre-writing, drafting, revising, editing, and publishing.

Once again, I reached a new milestone in my professional practice. My students were highly invested and engaged in their writing. Their pieces developed in vocabulary, syntax, and mature command of language. I began to see reciprocal benefits in their reading as well. Vocabulary development, inferential comprehension, and overall reader engagement were all fringe benefits of the pervasive enthusiasm about writing.

One of my fears was allayed when I realized my students were even learning to spell! It came as a welcome surprise when I discovered that, although they used invented spelling in their drafts, they ended the year passing a district-required, 100-word spelling test with a much greater success rate than my previous classes. My students wrote so frequently that their spelling of high-frequency words became consistent, and their desire to write more challenging words increased their attention to words in print.

For years, I continued to set aside time for a daily writing workshop and guided students through the writing process. Within the process, I learned that revision was the key to creating stronger writers. My students grew as authors when they stretched to improve their own compositions. While we didn't take every piece through the editing and publishing stages, we published for specific purposes—like contests, letters, and Mother's Day—or when students took pride in a piece and expressed a desire to publish it.

Side Effects of Accountability

Then along came testing, and perspectives shifted. Widespread accountability changed the face of writing instruction. There was no longer time to apply the writing process, and it was no longer safe to let children develop their own topics. The skills required by the test were the skills that became the centerpiece of classroom instruction, and the format of testing shaped the design of teaching.

Standardized achievement tests for reading and writing have been in existence for a long time. These tests can monitor student progress and indicate areas of weakness that can be addressed with intervention strategies. However, they have traditionally been delivered with considerable objectivity in multiple-choice formats.

While knowledge of conventions and terminology can be assessed by a multiple-choice format, actual writing proficiency cannot. The most authentic system for assessing the growth of the writer is the writing portfolio. Representative samples of student work can be collected over time to document writing development. However, portfolio assessment is subjective, time-consuming, and not nearly as efficient as the multiple-choice formats used for other disciplines.

In most states, standardized writing assessment was delivered in the form of a timed writing upon demand. For such a format, students are generally given a prompt and are expected to produce a genre-specific written response in a limited amount of time, usually somewhere between thirty and sixty minutes.

While such assessments are certainly efficient, they are just as certainly flawed. As with any standardized assessment, the weight placed upon outcomes creates a new operational context for schools and teachers, creating a pressure to alter their curriculum and methods to produce the desired test results.

A dangerous trend ensues. Rather than assessment informing instruction, instruction becomes aligned with the format and demands of the assessment. This danger moves the effect of standardized writing assessment from flawed to tragic. Consider the following problems of timed, prompted assessments:

Subjectivity of Holistic Scoring

Because the product being evaluated does not have definitive correct answers like multiple-choice reading and math exams, scoring is necessarily subjective. Generally, rubrics are employed to rate student responses along a continuum of quality. Scorers are trained to evaluate responses, but there is no way to ensure objectivity. In high-stakes testing, there should be no room for opinions. In some school systems, promotion/retention decisions are based on standardized writing scores. In many others, students are promoted but subjected to targeted intervention and remediation because of one writing sample at one sitting. How many good writers have been given low scores that are not indicative of their general fluency with written communication and had to endure unnecessary consequences?

The Erosion of Learner Attitudes

The high-stakes nature of testing and the resulting consequences often create an environment of fear and anxiety, and students begin to dread and dislike writing. As a teacher, I have watched simple interest inventories document a decline in attitudes toward the subject of writing. Over the years since the introduction of frequent timed, prompted assessments, I have observed a steady decline in the number of children who select writing as a favorite subject and a growing number who rank it at the bottom of their school day preferences. While teacher observations and informal interest inventories do not create measurable data recognized by school administrators and the greater educational community, scientific research regarding learner attitudes is emerging. Dr. Carolyn L. Piazza of Florida State University documented a downward spiral in high school students' attitudes toward writing (and a coinciding disregard for best practices in the teaching of writing). Piazza asserts that this affective lull should be viewed "within a wider historical-political context in which state assessments and predetermined standards potentially impact the kinds of instruction students are receiving." She and her associates have created a Writer's Disposition Scale (WDS) to measure the affective relationship between students and the discipline of writing (Heldref Publications, 2008). Why are learner attitudes important? Classroom teachers and education researchers agree: motivation, interest, and learner engagement are the essential intangibles of learning.

Dependence upon the Quality of the Prompt

When creating writing prompts for students, test developers must adhere to strict guidelines to avoid bias. For example, topics should avoid the mention of families or family members because there are students without families who may be adversely affected by the prompt and/or will have no experience from which to draw their content. Similarly, vacations, pets, certain weather conditions, and sports are off limits. Therefore, test developers are left with a shallow reservoir of topic possibilities. Prompts must be secure, so they are not usually recycled. As prompts are developed, psychometricians are often asked to review them to be sure they are as clear and direct as possible, communicating their intent with little chance for misinterpretation. However, even with such care built into their creation, prompts can be misleading and students can be completely befuddled, listening to the clock ticking away the time they are given to generate a complete and well-written essay. In some states, students are required to discern the mode of writing dictated by the prompt and respond in the appropriate format. With prompts varying from year to year, it is completely reasonable to assume that the overall quality of writing can be partially tied to the overall quality of the prompt. However, if scores drop from one year to the next, the typical response of school districts is to overhaul curriculum, methods, and even personnel.

The Tendency toward Formulaic Responses

Because schools and districts want the data to show that their students' achievement levels are climbing each year, they naturally begin to seek a formula for success. They extract writing skills from the state scoring rubric rather than decades of literature concerning best practices. They look for quick and easy systematic programs that promise the kind of success that is defined by scores. They hire consultants who guarantee a rise in scores. They implement periodic district- and school-level writing assessments to prepare students for the state exam. Soon, children lose an authentic sense of purpose and audience; the purpose of their writing becomes assessment and the audience becomes the scorer who will judge its value.

Students are afraid to take risks and be creative. Writing becomes uniform and formulaic. Teachers stop taking risks as well. They are afraid to explore genres that are not tested so that students will not become confused and write in the wrong mode. Sadly, in many situations, writing instruction becomes driven by the regular assignment of prompts that mimic the state assessment, and the same assessment-specific skills are drilled repeatedly. The litmus test for instructional decision making begins to shift from sound practice to the quest for superior achievement scores.

Truncating the Writing Process

Most tragic, perhaps, is that students no longer have the luxury of self-selected topics, personal expression, inspiration, and experiencing the writing process. The writing process has devolved in many classrooms to encompass only two steps: planning and drafting. Students are taught prescribed formats for planning. Rather than authentic pre-writing that involves discussion, brainstorming, research, and data collection, students are given prefabricated graphic organizers and asked to complete them in one brief sitting. They write rough drafts and are told to read them over once to correct mistakes. There is no time for meaningful conferencing and the kind of revision that cultivates reflective writers who invest themselves in the process of creating art with their words. Rather than communicating from the depth of their experiences with meaningful, self-selected topics, students write only in response to prompts. When this happens, we are creating responders, not writers. Students cease to realize that they have something of value to say to the world, and this is the critical moment when writing changes from a *process*-oriented to a *product*-oriented discipline.

Although flawed and damaging, accountability did something positive, however. It caused a lot of attention to be focused on writing. Teachers who may not have devoted much time to writing instruction in the past were giving the discipline a new priority. Publishers were producing instructional materials for writing and educators began to ask an important question.

How Do Children Learn to Write?

Learning to write is a developmental process that begins long before a child puts pencil to paper. Early writing begins with language acquisition. It is in the give and take of conversation that a child realizes that words transmit meaning. At first, the audience is the listener; later, the audience becomes the reader.

Basic language processes include listening, speaking, reading, and writing. These processes can be grouped as parallels. Listening and reading are both receptive processes through which we receive language and create meaning. Speaking and writing are expressive language processes by which we transmit meaning to others.

When viewing language in this integrated fashion, we can understand how oral language development in primary years forms the foundation of meaningful written communication during the school years. If we want to teach writing effectively, we must also understand how the development of writing proficiency parallels the development of speech.

Early babbling and imitation of sounds are to speech development what random scribbling and drawing are to writing development. As children grow, they play with words. In early speech development, they move from cooing and imitation to inventing pronunciations and terminology (*baba* for bottle and *boom boom* for bulldozer) to connecting words to form phrases (*play outside* and *go bye-bye now*).

Similarly, as they grow, children play with written language. As emergent writers, they move from scribbling and stringing a random sequence of letters together to inventing their own spelling as they learn to make letter-sound associations. As their interactions with written language increase, they begin to assimilate and internalize spelling and language conventions to become fluent writers.

Writing is rooted not only in oral language development, but also in the child's ability to make the connection of speech to print. Print surrounds us. Students begin to "read" environmental print when they relate symbols and fonts to restaurants and stores long before they can decode those names. As they grow, a language-rich environment filled with songs, poems, words, and books encourages children to continue making connections between the written and spoken word.

When we read aloud to a child, we demonstrate the speech-to-print connection. We expand vocabulary and explore the many ways that written words create meaning. By reading frequently, we model not only reading fluency and prosody, but also author's craft and the rhythm of language that students draw upon when writing. Most of us do not learn to recognize a complete sentence by diagramming it; rather, we recognize its completeness by the way it sounds.

Another way to group language processes is as reciprocals—listening and speaking are inverse processes, as are reading and writing. When a child accomplishes the abstract task of constructing meaning as a listener, she realizes the power of the spoken word. When a child utters *Mama* and the mother responds, the child experiences her own power of communication.

Similarly, reading and writing skills reciprocate each other. Before formal writing begins, most children find a way to write. Whether it's marker on paper or crayons on walls, the seemingly random scribbles of a toddler are the precursor to written communication. Through these random scribbles, children imitate the writing of adults and announce that they have joined the communication game.

When we learn to appreciate the inverse nature of reading and writing, we can consciously use them to feed and build each other. Emergent writers practice making letter-sound associations and writing with approximate spelling. The insightful teacher can informally assess the child's phonetic fluency by the approximations made.

As children grow and develop into more mature readers and writers, the more complex elements of craft become the focal point. A child whose writing contains imagery, literary devices, and clues for inference is a child who can certainly make inferences and build cognitive constructs needed for implicit comprehension of text.

Stages of Writing Development

Like speaking, writing is a developmental process. Children progress through clearly defined stages. Sometimes they cross back and forth between stages, and they very often exhibit elements of two stages at once. Compare this crossover to children as they learn to walk. They generally do not stop crawling the moment they have taken their first steps, but vary between crawling and walking for quite some time. This fluid acquisition is a natural part of any developmental process.

Descriptions of the general stages of writing development follow.

Drawing and Scribbling

Children learn that they can manipulate writing tools to create meaning. At this stage, it is important for children to have easy access to appropriate writing materials.

DYLAN, AGE TWO

Letter-like Forms

As children observe print in their environments and seek to mimic adults who model written communication, they create letter-like forms to represent meaning.

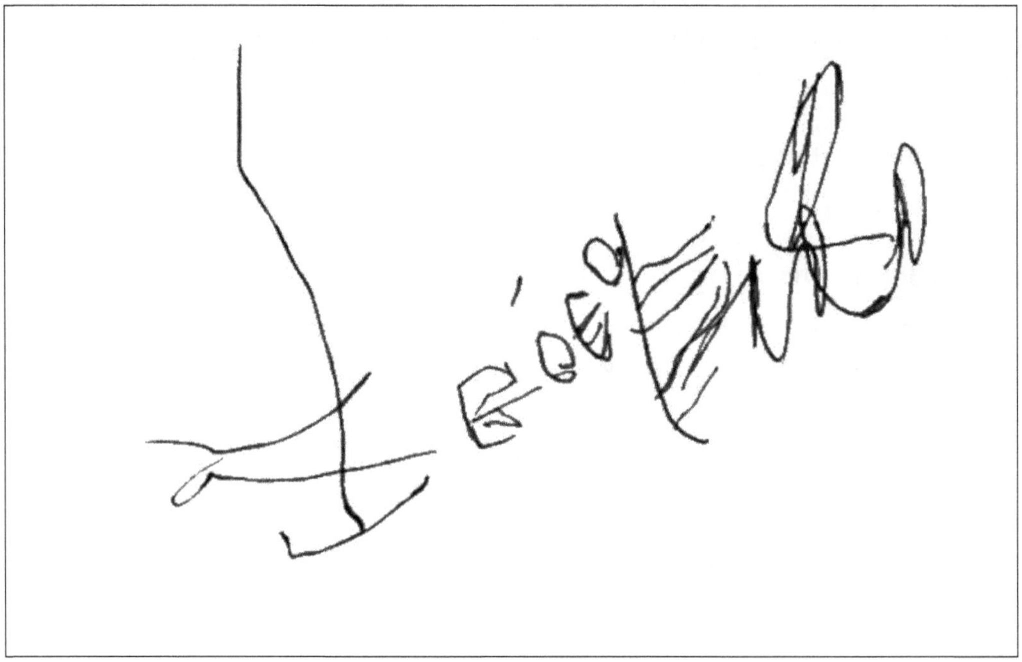

EMILY, AGE THREE

Random-letter Strings

Once students begin to learn letter formations and understand that those letters combine to make words, they will write random strings of letters and, in the time period immediately following the writing, can probably "read" to the listener the intended meaning.

EMILY, AGE FOUR

Spelling Approximations

As students acquire knowledge about the alphabetic principal, they learn to make letter-sound associations and put letters together as intentional representations of spoken words. It is at this stage teachers can begin to glean valuable information about a child's overall progress toward literacy.

Students generally begin with isolated initial-sound representations:

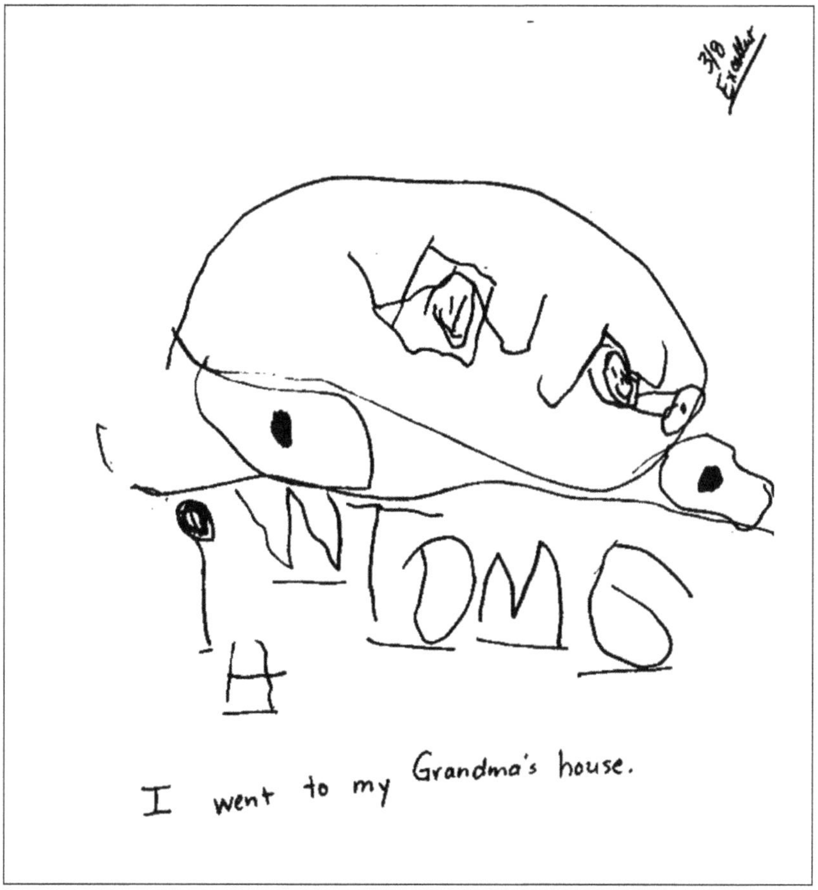

HILLARY, AGE FOUR

Teacher Analysis: Although there is an absence of capitalization, punctuation, and spelling, this child exhibits a working knowledge of left-to-right progression and text wrap—elements of written language that Marie Clay calls "concepts of print" (Heinemann, 1975). While most words are recorded by initial sounds only, the high-frequency word "to" has already been internalized as part of the child's writing (and therefore reading) repertoire. This child's understanding of the concepts of print is indicative of frequent exposure to literature.

As their ability to discriminate individual sounds in words increases, children add final consonants:

EMILY, AGE FIVE

Teacher Analysis: This child has developed facility with some conventions, including word spacing, text wrap, and end marks. While she has internalized the spelling of several high-frequency words, her spelling approximations for unknown words (i.e, "bek yid" for "back yard" and "sweg" for "swinging") indicates knowledge of beginning and ending consonants, and a readiness to develop proficiency with medial vowel sounds. As a reader, this child is probably able to identify several high-frequency words in print while using beginning sounds and illustrations to predict unknown words.

And finally, children's ability to identify medial vowels and multiple syllables generally coincides with reading readiness:

HILLARY, AGE FIVE

Conventional Spelling

As they gain experience with reading and writing, students internalize the spelling of words they frequently see and/or seek to spell. Throughout our lives, most of us continue adding to our vocabularies and learning the conventional spelling of words as we interact with them.

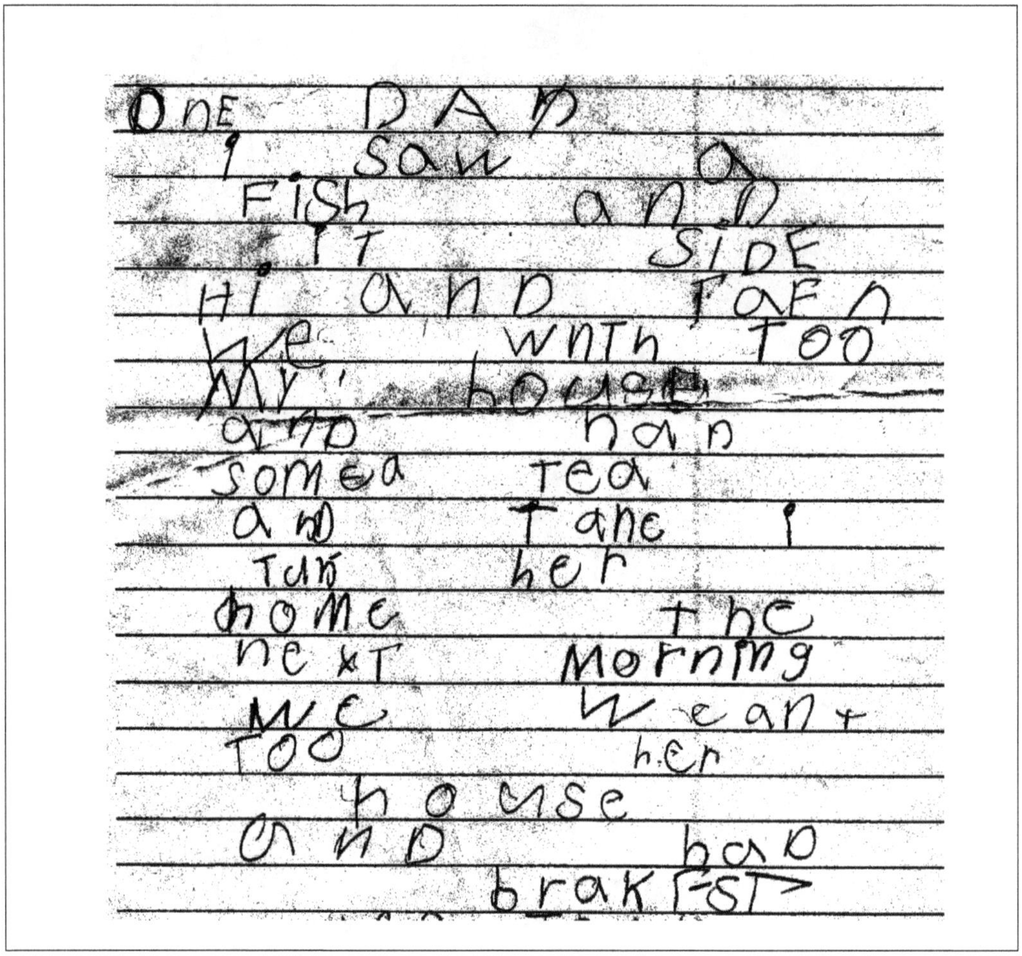

DYLAN, AGE SIX

"One day I saw a fish and it said, 'Hi,' and then we went to my house and had some tea, and then I took her home. The next morning we went to her house and had breakfast."

Teacher Analysis: This child has moved beyond a focus on sounds, words, and sentences and toward a focus on story. It is at this point we can begin to shift the focus of writing instruction from applied phonics and facility with print concepts to an introduction of craft skills that will enhance the child's blossoming literacy development

Implications for Teaching and Learning

We cannot expect school-age children to meet "grade-level standards" for writing if they do not possess adequate development in all language processes. Therefore, we must approach literacy instruction in a well-integrated fashion and consider the following implications for learning:

- Reading aloud to children should begin in infancy and continue well beyond the time children become independent readers.
- Toddlers should have ready, consistent access to books and appropriate writing materials to facilitate their progress through the stages of writing development.
- Emergent writers should dwell in a language-rich environment and should practice "applied phonics" by making letter-sound associations to create spelling approximations.
- Emergent writers should be able to develop their writing skills in a risk-free environment, where the focus is on communication rather than language mechanics.
- Due to the reciprocal nature of language processes, instruction in reading and writing should be integrated, especially during the primary years.
- Frequent exposure to high-quality children's literature is necessary for building a foundation in vocabulary, syntax, higher-order comprehension, prosody and the rhythm of language, as well as learner engagement.
- When students are ready to begin composing complete pieces, our focus on craft should begin with the introduction of descriptive writing skills that build the substance of their written expressions. The emphasis becomes the message and its meaningful delivery to the reader.

How Are Children Being Taught to Write?

We can probably all agree that children should be taught to write and that teachers should dedicate instructional time to the teaching of writing. However, we may differ in our ideas of *how* writing should be taught and *how often* students should be writing.

As we discussed earlier, most states require some form of statewide writing assessment. This ensures that writing standards are addressed in state and district curriculum plans. Some states have adopted curricula for writing, and some districts have developed their own formative writing assessments to monitor progress and make sure students are on the writing achievement track.

On paper, this looks like an effective accountability plan. However, for the classroom teacher and the individual student, what does this mean? What types of interaction between teacher and student actually promote the student's development into someone proficient in written communication?

Echoing a theme he has repeated over many years, author Donald H. Graves writes, "Children express themselves easily in first grade but gradually lose that creative freshness" (Heinemann, 1994). What happens after those primary years, when writing is engaging and flows naturally? Why do children lose that *creative freshness*?

We need to examine years of writing instruction and glean from it the effective instructional practices that develop students as writers without turning them into producers of uniform responses that lack that creative freshness Graves identified.

The teaching of writing has evolved from a component of language arts to a stand-alone core curriculum area. In *Building a Writing Community* (Maupin House, 2003), Marcia Freeman chronicles the history of writing education in elementary schools as follows:

Assume, Assign, and Assess
If you can read, you can write.

Creative Writing Journals
Assumption: *Story is important.*

Writing Process
What writers DO.

Writing Craft
What writers KNOW.

Writing craft provided teachers with a concrete, skills-based writing curriculum on which to build instruction. We seemed to be moving in a new direction toward mastery of achievable objectives that could elevate the level of any piece of writing.

However, the focus on individual craft skills taught in isolation only embellished formulaic writing pieces. A sprinkling of strong verbs, similes, and onomatopoeia throughout a formulaic response merely decorated the writing rather than truly improving it. Writing skills can be taught and practiced in isolation, but to be truly effective, they must be applied in a meaningful context. To join these writing-craft skills with writing process seemed inevitable.

Doing What Makes Sense

For a while, I allowed myself to tread a path of weak resignation toward practices that served accountability requirements over sound literacy development. Although I knew the value of great literature and the joy experienced from taking pride in a well-crafted piece of writing, born of the author's struggle to find the right words, the right images, and the right rhythm, I allowed my practice to change.

My students had to learn to pass the test. There wasn't time for development. Learning had to occur on a tight schedule. When my district instituted timed writing assessments each quarter—beginning in first grade—organization and beginning-to-end progression took precedence over the development of message, voice, and descriptive writing.

Because these assessments were designed as responses to written prompts, all motivation and inspiration were coming from outside the child. The message and purpose were contrived. The first step in assessing the child's writing proficiency was the confirmation that the response was "on topic."

At one point, during the advent of writing assessment, I remember being in a district workshop where we were instructed that student responses were to be considered off topic, and therefore unscoreable, if students did not mention key words from the prompt in the first sentence.

My immediate reaction was one of internal rebellion. In such a rigid, prompt-driven world, Herman Melville's teacher may have forced him to replace his famous opening line, *Call me Ishmael*, with a more on-topic *This is a story about a man obsessed with chasing a whale.*

As time passed, the district softened up on some of its sillier mandates. They discovered the value of clever leads and implied topics. As they relented, so did I, and at some point we met in the middle and joined forces in championing uniformity and blandness. However, I couldn't remain in that role. I experienced a growing sense of dissatisfaction with my own practice.

Teaching writing, which had once been a joyful experience for me, left me feeling sad, unfulfilled and, finally, repentant. It didn't help that my students *hated* writing. So I reached back into my memories and retrieved the writing process, writer's workshop, self-selected topics, and portfolios. And to those, I added explicit instruction in writing craft.

Criticism of the process approach to teaching writing pointed to the lack of systematic skill instruction. Generally, in a writing-process approach, skills are taught incidentally, as they are drawn from student writing. There is not a master plan of skills to be taught, mastered, and built upon. When teaching writing craft, the skills are identified in advance and explicitly taught.

In *Building a Writing Community*, Marcia Freeman tells us:

> *Using the writing process without teaching writing craft is an ineffectual exercise. It is equivalent to presenting kids with the rules and process of conducting a game of baseball, having them play, but never teaching and coaching the skills of hitting, throwing, catching, pitching, base running, bunting, and fielding.* (p. 6)

When I began to teach craft skills in a daily workshop environment, I rediscovered the pleasure of teaching writing, and my students discovered that they were skilled writers with something meaningful to say. We truly became a community of writers—thinking, creating, revising, and sharing. My students performed well on writing assessments, but the rubric score assigned to their writing began to matter less and less to them. They were setting their own standards.

With a comprehensive collection of writing-craft skills and knowledge of the writing process, we can combine the best of what we know from the past and the present to create a substantive writing workshop. In this book, you will find a detailed picture of the craft-centered daily writing workshop (*what to do*) and a list of writing-craft skills that form the content of writing instruction (*what to teach*). You will discover that you can be systematic and thorough in your teaching without sacrificing creativity. And your students will discover that they are writers.

Chapter Two
The Writing Process

"We are coaches, encouragers, developers, creators of environments in which our students can experience the writing process for themselves." (p. 5)

—Donald Murray, "Teach Writing as a Process, Not a Product," The Leaflet

What Is the Writing Process?

The writing process has been a widely accepted and broadly applied structure within the writing classroom for many years. The process recognizes that authors do not generate literary masterpieces by rapidly moving words from idea to paper in one continuous flow. Instead, a written piece is built by working through a series of steps:

- Pre-writing
- Rough draft
- Revision
- Editing
- Publishing

Pre-writing

Before defining what pre-writing *is*, we should establish what it *is not*. Pre-writing *is not* providing students with a graphic organizer and expecting them to quickly form a well-sequenced, cohesive plan for a written piece. We must teach and model the *thinking* that takes place before they put pencil to paper. Students must learn to *think like writers*.

Lucy Calkins writes about "living the writerly life" in *The Art of Teaching Writing* (Heinemann, 1994). She chronicles the way several accomplished authors ignite inspiration and collect details that surface in their writings. She discusses the way Karla Kuskin gathers sensory fragments from her daily experiences and they become her catalysts for writing. Calkins notes that Betsy Byars saves cuttings that pique her interest from photographs and clippings and stores them in a dresser drawer. Calkins concludes:

> *Rehearsal for writing* can *involve brainstorming possible topics or mapping possible directions for a piece, but the more important thing is that students realize rehearsal involves living wide-awake lives—seeing, hearing, noticing, wondering—and gathering all of this in bureau drawers or notebooks or daybooks.*

Young writers must develop the ability to be keen observers of details in their environments, psychically categorizing information, emotions, ideas, and sensory experiences. They must learn to nourish ideas in their minds, opening mental file folders and linking the related information, emotions, ideas, and sensory experiences until the ideas become ripe for writing.

Sometimes the details must be sought with intention. Writers need to conduct research and gather data. The process of conducting research is something that must be taught, modeled, and guided. Research involves locating appropriate sources, discerning reliable from unreliable sources, determining which details are pertinent to the topic, and eliminating extraneous information.

Pre-writing includes thinking, discussing, researching, sketching, and organizing. This is the time when an author generates an idea, builds upon it, structures it, and attaches words to the idea. Usually, in addition to brainstorming and reading, this process involves talking.

Verbalizing an idea allows the author to sequence events or information and move the idea from the abstract toward the concrete. When discussing an idea with a peer or small group, the author is able to bounce ideas off of willing listeners and ponder the questions that arise. This refining process provides the foundation for sound structure within the written piece.

After students have invested in concept development and mental organization, they can jot down their ideas on a graphic organizer. This organizer becomes the road map for a piece of writing, ensuring that the author doesn't veer off course or inadvertently omit important details, events, or information.

I recommend uncomplicated organizers and often have students fold or draw lines to create their own graphic organizers rather than duplicating prefabricated planning sheets. If you and your students feel more comfortable with a template for planning, several genre-specific graphic organizers are included in the **Appendix**.

Most writing can simply begin with lists. Listing is a foundational skill that can begin in preschool: *Let's list the things we've done today; we will make a list of all the red items we can find in the classroom; let's list everything we can think of that begins with the sound /f/.* Listing is a primary organizational skill that supports *focus* for writers of all ages.

When constructing the framework for a narrative piece, young writers must think along a linear plot line, listing main events in the order in which they will occur in the story. Sometimes the list of main events must be modified to give the story a logical flow. Sometimes the student must determine the final outcome in a story and work backwards through the events leading up to that outcome.

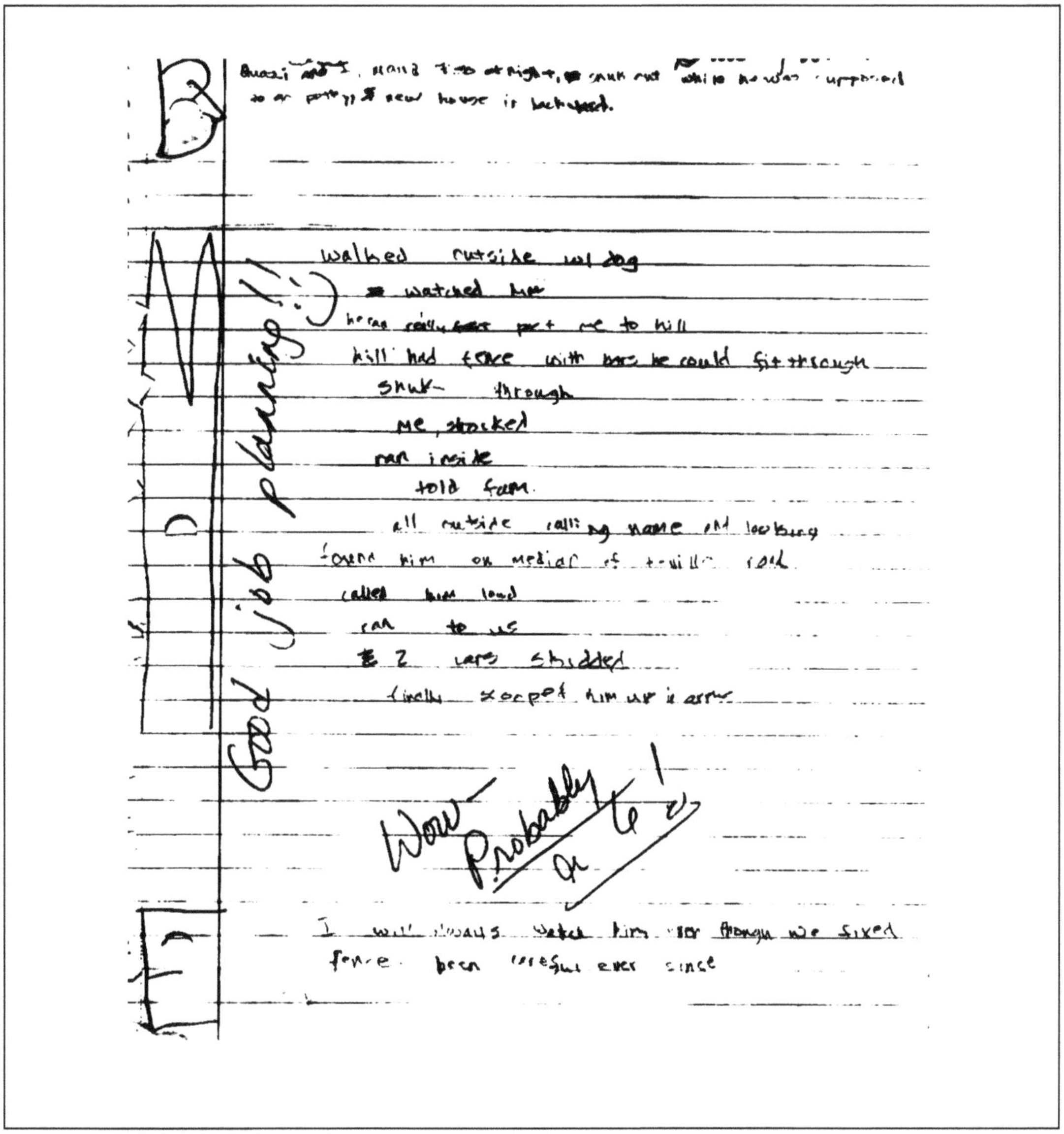

PERSONAL NARRATIVE PLAN - BRITTANY, FIFTH GRADE

For detail-rich expository writing, students should begin by listing a wealth of details related to the topic without adhering to a particular order. The items on these randomly assorted lists of details can be grouped to organize the content of the body paragraphs. As groups of related details are formed, the focus of the piece begins to emerge. This is the natural process of writing—a collection of ideas that begins to shape the piece.

Marcia Freeman calls this process "list-linking." By beginning with details, students shape their writing focus and build organization from the bottom up. Related details can be identified by color-coding (*all blue-highlighted details go together in one paragraph; all yellow highlighted details go together in a paragraph*) or by geometric sorting (*one set of related details is marked with a triangle; another set is marked with a square; a third set is marked with a circle*).

Students can create their own icons for groups of related details:

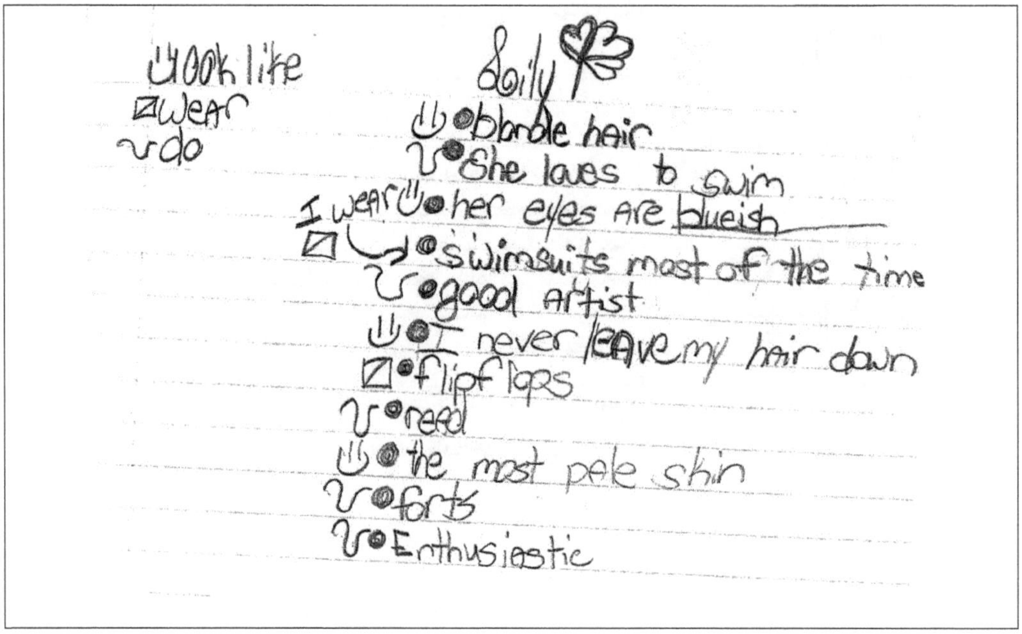

LIST-LINKING: GEOMETRIC SORTING – LILY, FOURTH GRADE

Expository organizers should allow students to group related details together and can include concept webs, semantic maps, and boxed flow charts.

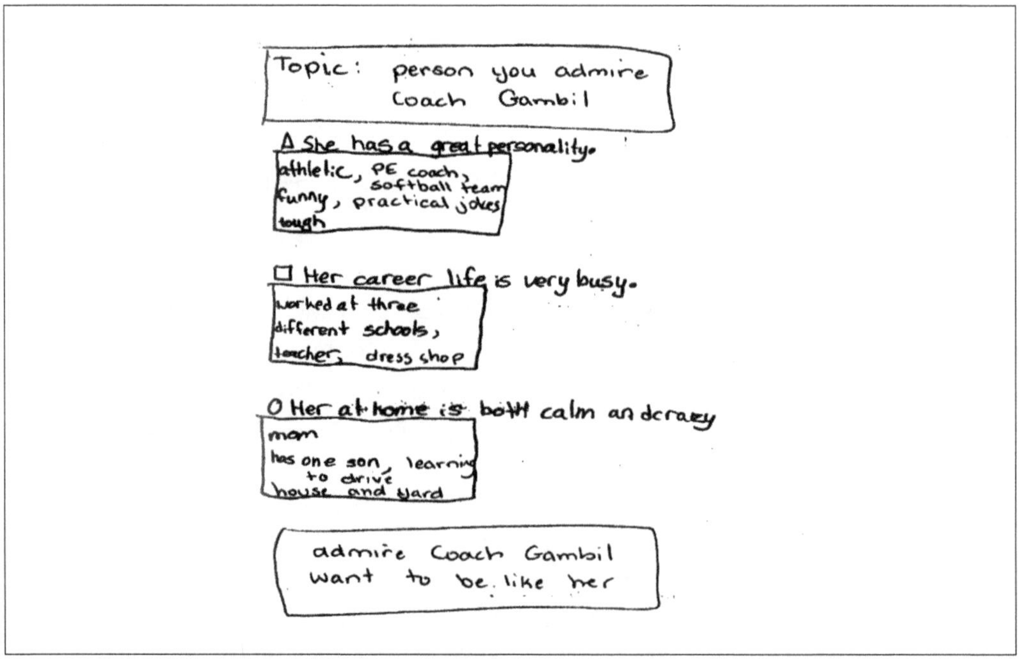

EXPOSITORY BOXED FLOW CHART – BRYNN, FIFTH GRADE

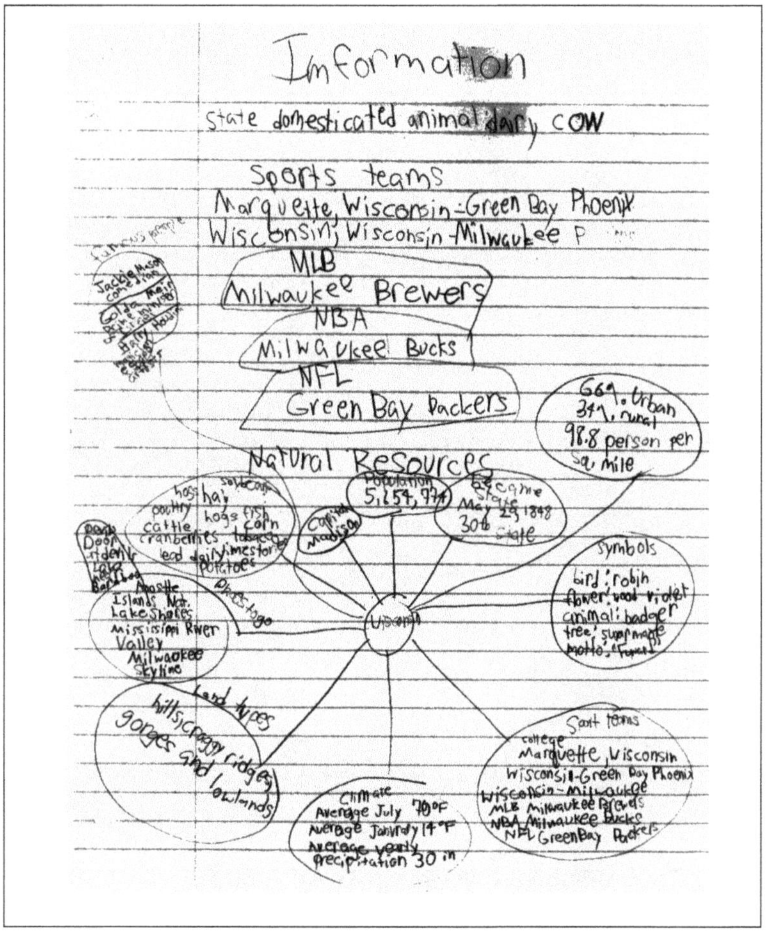

CONCEPT WEB – JAKE, FOURTH GRADE

When making comparisons between two or more objects, lists are very effective ways to juxtapose attributes.

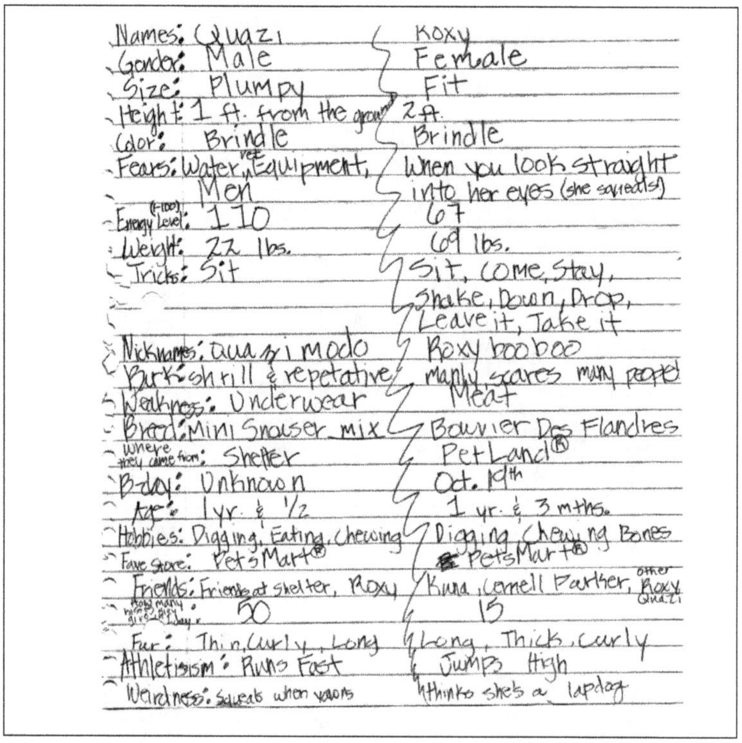

Names:	Quazi	Roxy
Gender:	Male	Female
Size:	Plumpy	Fit
Height:	1 ft. from the ground	2 ft.
Color:	Brindle	Brindle
Fears:	Water, vet Equipment, Men	When you look straight into her eyes (she squeals!)
Energy Level: (1-100)	110	67
Weight:	22 lbs.	69 lbs.
Tricks:	Sit	Sit, come, Stay, Shake, Down, Drop, Leave it, Take it
Nicknames:	Quazimodo	Roxy booboo
Bark:	shrill & repetative	manly scares many people
Weakness:	Underwear	Meat
Breed:	Mini Snauser mix	Bouvier Des Flandres
Where they came from:	Shelter	PetLand®
B-day:	Unknown	Oct. 19th
Age:	1 yr. & 1/2	1 yr. & 3 mths.
Hobbies:	Digging, Eating, chewing	Digging, Chewing Bones
Fave Store:	PetsMart®	PetsMart®
Friends:	Friends at shelter, Roxy	Kina, Cornell Parker, other Roxy Quazi
How many times a day:	50	15
Fur:	Thin, Curly, Long	Long, Thick, curly
Athletisism:	Runs Fast	Jumps High
Weirdness:	Squeals when yawns	thinks she's a lapdog

COMPARISON LIST: COMPARING TWO DOGS BY ATTRIBUTES - BRITTANY, FIFTH GRADE

Sometimes, pre-writing involves sketching. Creating a storyboard—drawing a sequence of events on a paper folded to form boxes—can often assist younger writers in sequencing events, and sketches can be an aid to older students in visualizing. An author must be able to picture scenes and their inherent details in order to write in a way that leads the reader toward visualization.

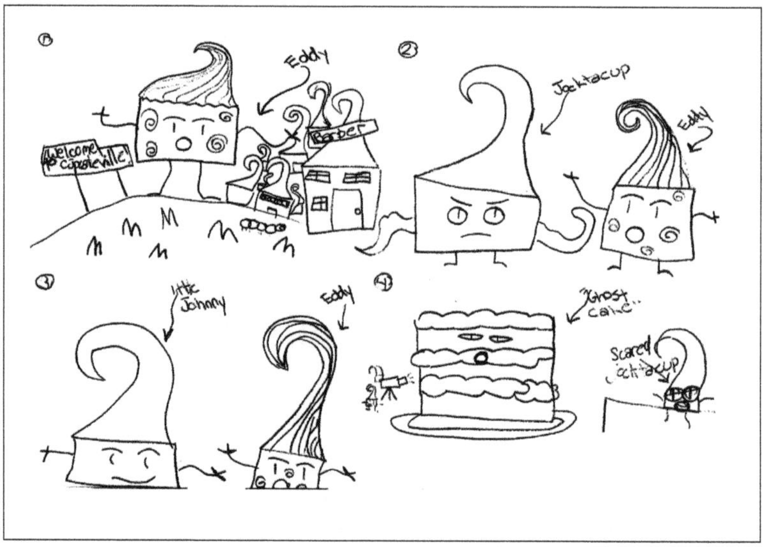

STORYBOARD, NARRATIVE ORGANIZER - LILY, FOURTH GRADE

Pre-writing, as it is described previously, does not fit into the timed writing-upon-demand assessment format. Many teachers and administrators feel more comfortable when children are restricted to practicing in the format that will be presented on "the test." With high stakes and professional reputations attached to test scores, this is understandable.

However, students who develop the ability to *think like writers*—who have been given ample opportunities to practice the pre-writing stage of the process—can usually generate a plan for a substantive piece within the time constraints of assessments. Students who have been restricted to quickly and quietly filling in graphic organizers will not be able to *think like writers*. They have been trained to follow a formula.

This doesn't mean we should never allow students to practice a test format. Of course, we don't want the format to be a variable that hasn't been experienced and can impede students from performing to the best of their abilities. It is entirely appropriate to allow students to practice the pre-writing format of a standardized test when the test is approaching. However, this format should not be standard practice.

Drafting

Once students have invested in the thinking and planning that forms the foundation of a written piece, they are ready to begin drafting. A rough draft is the pouring forth of ideas onto to the page, allowing the piece to emerge from the plan. Some writers like to plow through a draft, getting the basis of the piece written so they can go back and carefully revise. Others like to continually revise as the draft is being written.

Many pieces are written for the purpose of practice and instruction, never moving beyond the draft stage. Some drafts may lay dormant until a student decides to carry them further. In any case, these pieces should not be called *finished pieces* because they have not been revised. They have a beginning, a middle, and an end and may be bursting with potential, but until completing the writing process, they should be referred to as *drafts*.

Drafts do not always have to be long pieces. When we're teaching elements of craft, students should be allowed to apply new skills in brief practice pieces. These pieces can be easily shared, and the skills are readily identified.

Mom

Her irresistable, unconditional love keeps my heart whole

warm, hazel eyes shoot beems of happiness
into the sorrow filled world
constant, helpful encouragement congratulates me in
everything I do
welcoming smile charms anyone who
deserves it and her
binding trust glues us together.

DRAFT OF DESCRIPTIVE PIECE APPLYING CHARACTER TRAITS - ERIN, FIFTH GRADE

If you use writing warm-ups in your classroom, you are allowing your students to apply skills in brief draft form on a regular basis. Sometimes, you will find that students are able to pluck literary gems from these warm-ups and apply them in larger pieces, or they may be able to develop full pieces from the brief draft created during a warm-up.

When students are allowed to journal or "free-write," most will begin to develop several different drafts. Many of these pieces may lay dormant. Some may go unfinished because another idea came along. Some may be revisited and may become polished, published pieces. In all cases, students are practicing and applying their writing skills by creating drafts.

Modern students are very experienced at writing rough drafts. As discussed in the first chapter, writing assessments halt at the draft. In most testing situations, students are asked to generate a plan and a complete piece of writing within a set time limit. Although they may reserve a few minutes to read over the piece for the purpose of editing and revision, they are writing a draft.

While assessments may be halted at the draft, we cannot relegate our instruction and expectations to this unpolished state. Although many pieces will remain drafts written for the purpose of practice, some pieces must be selected for revision. It is in revising that students *move the target* of their own skill and expectations.

Revising

"Unless you try to do something beyond what you have already mastered, you will never grow."

— Ralph Waldo Emerson

Revision is probably the most valuable process we can teach our students—and probably the one most difficult and least often applied. Children do not want to revise; they want to be finished. However, it is in the process of revision that young writers learn the extent of their potential. Revision moves the target of writing expectations and accomplishment.

The two main purposes for revising are to improve *clarity* and *interest*. The reader must be able to understand the concepts or story line being presented without lingering questions that impede comprehension and deteriorate the reader's enjoyment of the text.

Revising for interest is an appeal to the aesthetics of literary techniques. As writers, we want our language to interest our readers. We strive for precision in our word choices and seek to help the reader visualize and connect to the text.

When our writing instruction is based on the skills of writing craft, we have tools that make revision a more concrete endeavor. We are not merely telling young authors to go back and "make it better." Instead, we suggest strong verbs to assist the reader in visualizing and specificity to help the reader connect to the text. We offer the idea that a particular beginning technique will pull the reader into the story from the very beginning.

These concrete suggestions are easily understood by students and readily applied by teachers when the content of craft is the basis of writing instruction. A student can add a compelling lead (*Ding! The silver bell rang to let Trudy know that the first customer of the day had come into the store.*) and scan the piece for verbs to strengthen (*rushed* instead of *came*) and general nouns that can be made specific (*Betty's Cash and Carry* instead of *the store*).

Marcia Freeman suggests that teachers use the phrase *Your Reader* instead of the word *I* when conferencing with students about revisions: *Your reader might wonder why everyone is staring at the main character; some visual details would help your reader build a picture of the character and connect with the startled bystanders.* This small shift in verbiage broadens the scope of the audience for the young author—and every writer must realize there is an audience beyond the teacher.

Many teachers try to hold formal writing conferences with each student, reviewing a rough draft with a fine-tooth comb and making many suggestions for improvements. However, students will probably gain more value from the revision process if they can take ownership over it. Provide no more than three focused suggestions. Beyond three, your students may begin to feel defeated and overwhelmed, which will only be counterproductive. Therefore, be brief and focused in your conferencing, and give students tools for independence.

The most efficient process I have found is to circulate and hold on-the-spot conferences while students are working. Teachers of emergent writers may be able to hold conferences with each student because of the brevity of their written pieces. With older students who write lengthier pieces, you can skim and spot-check pieces for logic, flow, and writing craft. After a brief discussion, give students a checklist of the skills for which they should revise and have them follow a self-guided revision tour, reading for multiple skills at once.

When you have been teaching specific writing-craft skills, you can set your expectations in advance and let students know what is required of them. With young students, be very direct: *I expect to see that you have used onomatopoeia as a beginning technique, at least three time-order transitions, at least five strong verbs, one simile, and a feeling statement as an ending technique.* Setting these types of expectations facilitates the application of skills you have taught, provides a concrete foundation for revision and self-evaluation, and adds objectivity to the scoring process.

With older students, the expectations may be broader and less specific but still add objectivity and concreteness to the writing process: *I expect to see well-crafted beginning and ending techniques; examples of personification, metaphors, and similes; strong verbs throughout the piece; appropriate transitional devices; and clues for inference.* To self-evaluate, have students highlight these skills in their rough drafts or complete a checklist like the following samples, quoting their own work to identify skills employed.

Sample Self-evaluation Revision Worksheet for Younger Writers

Author's Name: ____

Title of Piece: ____

Check to be sure you have included each of the following required skills in your piece.

_____ I began my piece with ONOMATOPOEIA:

_____ I used these TIME ORDER TRANSITIONS:

1.
2.
3.

_____ I used these STRONG VERBS:

1.
2.
3.
4.
5.

_____ This is the FEELINGS STATEMENT at the end of my piece:

You can design your own revision worksheet to fit your instructional focus. However, requiring young writers to "fill in the blanks" with examples of the craft skills applied in their pieces ensures a much more scrupulous re-reading process than a standard checklist. See the **Appendix** for a reproducible revision worksheet you can use in your classroom.

More mature writers do not usually require the careful guidance needed by young writers during the revision process. Older students are generally motivated by meeting the assignment criteria. Therefore, a checklist can help assure that these mature writers have included the skills for which you are holding them accountable.

Sample Self-evaluation for Intermediate/Secondary Writers

Author's Name: ____

Title of Piece: ____

Read your rough draft. Put a check by each writing-craft skill as you find it, and highlight the craft in your rough draft. If you don't find these skills in your piece, revise to add them.

____ Beginning technique

____ Transitional devices

____ Personification

____ Metaphor

____ Simile

____ Strong verbs (Count at least ten strong verbs in your piece)

____ Clues for inference

____ Ending technique

Read your rough draft again and check for the following:

____ Word choice is precise and varied.

____ It makes sense. The reader can follow the text and understand it.

Sometimes setting expectations and providing checklists will be enough to ensure that students are practicing the application of writing-craft skills you have taught. You can collect and assess these pieces and move along to another writing project. At other times, you will want to use this type of checklist as a springboard for further revisions.

When revising pieces to continue the writing process toward editing and publishing, be sure that students are given ample time to receive substantive feedback. Realistically, we cannot afford the classroom time to read every complete piece and hold a meaningful conference with every student about those pieces. A more efficient and on-the-spot technique is to circulate and conference with students while they are writing. Additionally, teach students set procedures for peer conferencing. Peer conferences can be very valuable but can also be an opportunity for mayhem if procedures are not taught in advance. Specific procedural tips for peer conferences are discussed in more detail in **Chapter 3**.

Most likely, your students will not *want* to go back and revise their pieces after the last period is in place; you can count on that. However, providing the time, procedure, and language for revision will give them a greater sense of control. It is during the revision process that students truly grow as writers and move the target of their own expectation

Editing

Sometimes students confuse the steps of revision and editing. This is natural, since both take place largely after the rough draft is written (although mature writers will also continually re-read, revise, and edit *as they write*). While revision improves the clarity and interest of a piece, the focus of editing is on the accuracy of language conventions.

Language conventions include capitalization, punctuation, grammar, and spelling. These are not the fun and inspiring elements of the writing process; they are essential skills for publishing well-written pieces with clarity of intention and inherent credibility.

Without accuracy of language conventions, readers can become easily confused. Lynne Truss, author of the best-seller *Eats, Shoots & Leaves* (Gotham Books, 2003), pointed out with grace and humor the confusion created by improper use of punctuation:

> *"Punctuation has been defined many ways. Some grammarians use the analogy of stitching: punctuation as the basting that holds the fabric of language in shape. Another writer tells us that punctuation marks are the traffic signals of language: they tell us to slow down, notice this, take a detour, and stop....But best of all, I think, is the simple advice given by the style book of a national newspaper: that punctuation is 'a courtesy designed to help readers to understand a story without stumbling.'*
>
> *Isn't the analogy with good manners perfect? Truly good manners are invisible: they ease the way for others, without drawing attention to themselves."* (p. 7)

Like good manners, language conventions go largely unnoticed unless they are absent or wrongly applied. More often than I care to admit, my students have lovingly produced a card announcing, "*Your* the best teacher!" While the sentiment is sweet, what resonates in my consciousness is my need for additional lessons in proper use of the contraction, *you're*.

Even more confusing for the reader is the absence of capitalization and end punctuation. Actively teach young children to read their pieces aloud and listen for places where end punctuation is needed. Model the process with exaggerated inflections. Build an inherent sense of language flow that will not only assist them in properly placing end punctuation and beginning capitalization, but will also build their prosody and oral reading fluency.

As they mature and grow in their knowledge of language conventions, hold students accountable for the ever-expanding breadth of grammar and punctuation they have learned. Using their own work as a vehicle for applying grammar skills is far more powerful and effective than using prefabricated worksheets to practice those same skills.

Marcia Freeman, in *Building a Writing Community* (pp. 98-100), suggests teaching students to "edit by ear." Because most students have gained competency over the syntax of spoken language, they can *listen* for the places where language mechanics should be adjusted. She suggests training primary students to edit by ear through the use of teacher modeling.

In Freeman's procedure, students gather around a Big Book. The teacher chooses an editing skill (e.g., end punctuation) and exaggerates vocal inflections indicated by end punctuation as she reads chorally with the students. On a second reading, the teacher removes the text so that the children are not able to see it, and she reads it to them. Students are asked to cluck their tongues or snap their fingers to identify places where end punctuation belongs.

The process can be repeated with a student reading the text while others indicate places where end punctuation belongs. Once students learn the process, they can work in peer conferences to help each other edit written manuscripts. With more advanced students, the procedure can be modified to help students practice "hearing" where new paragraphs should begin.

In order to "hear" the need for punctuation and grammar changes in text, Freeman suggests teaching students to "murmur read" their pieces. She tells students to "read just loud enough for them to hear their voices, but not disturbing others" (p. 73). By speaking the text aloud, students not only engage their aural processes, but also slow their processing of the text by speaking it rather than reading it silently.

In my classroom, I often conduct a guided, layered group editing prior to circulating and conducting mini-conferences with individuals. During this multi-step procedure, I direct students to re-read their pieces several times, each time reading for a different purpose: *Read your piece carefully, focusing on capital letters. Be sure you have capitalized the beginning of each sentence, proper nouns, and the word "I."*

I continue this process, each time naming a different skill: *Now read your piece and make sure you have placed quotation marks around any dialogue being spoken by your characters. Now read for consistent tense. Now read for overused words. This time read for spelling. If you are not 100 percent sure that a word is spelled correctly, circle it.*

Whether there are two or ten steps in my editing process, I save spelling for the last step. After circling words, students can get out their dictionaries and use them to correct spelling. Spelling is an ongoing quest for many adults, so learning to use resources to correct spelling is an invaluable skill to teach our students.

Because some students will need to look up the spelling of only a few words and others will have a lengthy list, their "finish points" will be staggered. Therefore, I am able to circulate and hold mini-conferences to assist individuals with revisions.

With older students who write lengthier pieces, you may need to alter the procedure. You can give students a checklist of the skills for which they should revise and have them follow a self-guided revision tour, reading for multiple skills at once. Here is a sample editing checklist.

Editing Checklist

____ **Capitalization**

(beginning of each sentence, proper nouns, the word "I")

____ **Punctuation**

(period, exclamation mark, question mark, commas, quotation marks, apostrophes)

____ **Grammar**

(consistent tense, consistent point of view, make sure sentences are complete unless you purposely use a fragment)

____ **Spelling**

You will not need to require students to complete the editing process for every piece. This would be a surefire way to push them toward brief pieces that lack descriptive details, sentence variation, and interesting language. Instead, facilitate periodic revision. One full-length piece taken all the way through the stages of revising and editing is an honorable and realistic goal in a grading period. With younger students who write shorter pieces, select up to three pieces to take through the entire writing process each grading period.

Of course, the number of pieces to take through the editing process is largely dependent upon the ages and stages of your young writers. A kindergarten teacher may take only one piece through the editing process in an entire school year. A first-grade teacher might decide to begin editing a few pieces during the second semester of the year. Even then, the conventions for which students are editing may be limited to end punctuation and beginning capitalization.

By second grade, students usually begin to take command over a greater number of language conventions, including the spelling of high-frequency words, commas in a series, and quotation marks for dialogue. Third grade is usually where conventions for paragraphing become an expectation.

Traditionally, fourth grade is a transitional year in which students apply skills they have learned up to that point. With the expectations of rudimentary conventions behind them, students begin to learn about various types of sentence structures, active and passive voice, point of view, and advanced grammar topics. From fourth grade forward, language conventions are expanded, refined, and more broadly applied.

Of course, this general timeline is only a rule of thumb. As we have learned, writing is a developmental process, and every child will not reach the same milestones at the same age. As teachers, we must continually assess where our students are functioning and then determine the next step on the continuum of learning.

Keep in mind that as you select pieces for editing and hold students accountable for correcting language conventions in their own writing, you are putting research into action and teaching grammar in the most effective manner. The Alliance for Excellent Education (with the support of the Carnegie Corporation of New York) recently published *Writing Next: Effective Strategies to Improve Writing of Adolescents in Middle and High Schools* to examine effective practices in the teaching of writing. On the subject of grammar, the report states:

> *...a recent study (Fearn & Farnan,2005) found that teaching students to focus on the function and practical application of grammar within the context of writing (versus teaching grammar as an independent activity) produced strong and positive effects on students' writing.* (p. 21)

Countless lectures and isolated worksheets cannot compete with the learning gains achieved through practical application of grammar skills in a meaningful context. While the assessment of writing should focus on content and style, language conventions cannot be ignored when a piece of writing will become public. Use your time wisely and teach those skills through the editing process.

Publishing

> *"I write to hold what I find in my hands and declare it a treasure." (p. 7)*
>
> ***— Lucy Calkins, The Art of Teaching Writing***

Every author needs *purpose* and *audience*. These are two essential fuels for the writing engine that cannot be taught but can be provided. When we give students an audience for whom to write and a specific purpose for writing—whether to express gratitude, make a suggestion, or present information—we are giving them a real audience and an authentic purpose for writing. Create opportunities for your students to publish their pieces—meaning, of course, to make them *public*—for an audience outside of your classroom.

When students are writing for a specific audience and know that their work will be read or displayed, there is an inherent reason why editing must take place. If someone else will be reading it, language conventions should be followed. Likewise, they will want to revise their writing so that this "real" reader will find it clear and interesting.

In Chapter Two, we discussed the structure and expectations for a publishing project. But what are some ways to publish student writing, and how can we establish purpose?

Author's Chair

Designating a special chair for an author to sit and share his or her work is a simple but powerful nonverbal means of communicating a message central to your writing workshop: *You are an author.* Once children have adopted this identity, writing becomes more than an assignment; it becomes art.

The author's chair can be decorated with color and flair, or it can be a sign of maturity, like a rolling desk chair, tall stool, or director's chair. The important thing is that your students understand that it is set aside for the sharing of finished works. The author deserves attention and feedback from a respectful community of writers.

Simple Displays

Bulletin boards and trophy cases are ideal spots for displaying published pieces of writing. Illustrations to accompany the piece or photographs of the author can be displayed alongside the written work to attract attention. Place blue-ribbon award stickers or gold seals on pieces to be displayed, and send the message that this written work is of notable distinction.

Class Books

There is automatically a purpose for writing and a sense of audience when the pieces being written are going to be assembled in an anthology of work or form a collective piece.

Primary students can produce simple, one-page pieces that blend themselves easily into a big book the class can share. Place the book on your bookshelf with professionally published volumes and send a message that this work is a book of similar importance. The familiarity and sense of ownership arising in students will lead them to read the class-made book again and again.

Intermediate students can gain a sense of purpose and audience from a class anthology. Stress that their best work should be submitted and open the door to revision and editing conferences. Create a table of contents for the anthology and collect various types of pieces—poetry, essays, recipes, stories—differentiated to showcase the varied and broad spectrum of thinking and writing styles in your classroom.

Digital Displays

Students are surrounded by technology, and giving authentic purpose to digital tools available is often difficult. Allow students to publish their pieces as a digital slideshow, importing pictures or scanning illustrations. Sharing published works electronically, via your classroom projector or school website, can be highly gratifying and can create motivation for seeing a piece through the entire writing process.

Professionally Constructed Books

Many craft stores sell blank books that students can use to create an attractive hardcover book. Several companies provide the service of binding individual hardcover books that students have created. These projects can be great fundraisers or viable proposals for grants.

These books were produced as part of a school-wide publishing project in conjunction with Studentreasures®.

Authors' Conference

Arrange an authors' conference at your school. Look for local writing associations that may be willing to send local authors to your school at no cost. While they may not be famous and widely read, just knowing that these adult volunteers are fellow writers who have created finished products and possibly seen them published is exciting and motivational for children. These adults can listen to pieces written by your students and offer encouraging advice and praise.

Many well-known authors are happy to schedule school visits for a fee. Search funding possibilities, like grants, parent organizations, and local reading councils. You might be surprised how feasible it would be to bring an author to your school. Very often, several schools share the cost of bringing an author to their community for consecutive school visits. These authors will make a presentation but can also be asked to meet with a select group of student writers to discuss the writing process and view student work.

Online Magazines

Many safe, reliable websites will post student work, but you can create your own online magazine at your school site. Scholastic offers some online publishing opportunities for students on their website, and www.launchpadmag.com posts selected student writing and art work in online journals.

Be sure you have the appropriate permission for making student pieces available on the Internet. Usually, no more than the first name of a child will appear with works published in this manner. However, how exciting it is for a child to access his or her work from a home computer or send the link to relatives living far away so they can easily view it as well.

Assessment

While publishing has been the historical final stage of the writing process, we need to consider the role of assessment in modern education. Assessment has become an adjunct to the writing process in modern classrooms. Unlike real-world, authentic writing, many student compositions are written expressly for the purpose of assessment.

Teachers may embrace or bemoan the prominence of accountability, but assessment is a necessary component of a standards-based curriculum. We need to monitor and evaluate our students' progress, and we are responsible for facilitating the standardized assessments presented by our schools, districts, and states. For this reason, we must determine the types of assessment we *choose* to implement and prepare students for the types of assessments *required* of them.

Formats for Writing Assessment

There are many different ways to measure student achievement. Sometimes assessment formats are given to us and we have the task of preparing students to achieve in those given formats. However, most of us have some leverage in determining how we will measure student progress on a formative and summative basis in our classrooms.

As conscientious professionals, we need to be aware of our choices and determine what's best for our students and our teaching situations. When gauging progress and formulating grades, our two guiding questions should be:

- *What type of assessment is best to inform my instruction?*
- *What type of assessment will provide a sound and objective basis for indicating my students' growth and achievement?*

As you read about the following formats for assessment, consider each in light of these guiding questions. Empower yourself to make informed decisions about assessments that will best serve your students and your professional environment.

Yes/no. It's rare that "pass/fail" marks are used to assess writing, but this practice might be the best way to assess pieces when the goal is determining proficiency. Most standardized assessments of writing currently use rubrics with a spread of four to six levels of achievement.

While this type of system ranks students and puts them into achievement groups that fit the dictates of accountability quite well, schools and districts must draw a hard line to determine whether or not students meet minimum criteria. Students either fall above or below that cut line. Below the line, they are determined to need remediation and possibly retention. Above the line, they are deemed proficient. However, ranking students' level of achievement as writers becomes a slippery slope.

When determining levels of writing proficiency, we are unable to escape subjectivity. No matter how rigorous the training, a piece of writing that excels as the highest level of achievement to one scorer might be only above average to another. The variance of one point on a rubric might seem minimal to the assessor, but what does that point mean to the child?

Levels of achievement on standardized tests, applied to one prompted piece of writing by a stranger, seem to become black and white identity labels when printed on report cards and cumulative folders. The numbers precede the child and color the opinions of subsequent teachers as well as the child's opinion of himself.

These scores impose a stigma, and some children have great difficulty overcoming the emotional attachment to the quantitative assessment of their writing. The only determination we really need to make with standardized writing assessments is whether or not students are effective with written communication. Sometimes a simple "yes" or "no" is all that's necessary. Why stratify the levels and label the students with this one snapshot?

In the classroom, a pass/fail method of assessing writing may not be a useful or appropriate scoring tool for most writing situations. However, when determining whether or not students have grasped a writing skill well enough for you to move on to a new skill, a quick "yes" or "no" may suffice.

Student writes with a sense of completeness, clarity of message, adequate support, logical flow of ideas, and an age-appropriate command of language conventions:

______Yes ______No

Holistic scoring. Because the discipline of writing is open to opinion and artistic choices, holistic scoring has become very popular in the assessment of writing. As its name suggests, holistic scoring provides a way to look at the *whole* rather than dissecting a composition into parts or focusing too narrowly on one element of writing.

The idea behind holistic scoring is that the product makes its impression on the reader in its entirety; in other words, *the whole is greater than the sum of its parts.* Rubrics for holistic scoring are easily available, generally ranging from a point range of three to six levels.

Holistic scoring systems usually include broad elements of writing to guide the scorer in evaluating the piece. Generally, style, organization, and language conventions are included in these elements. Sometimes readers are also asked to evaluate support, word choice, usage, or voice.

Most standardized writing assessments are scored holistically, and if your students are required to demonstrate their writing achievement based on the elements of a state rubric, you will need to familiarize your students with the specific elements and levels included in your district or state scoring system.

Holistic scoring is very useful in assessing the overall effectiveness of a piece of writing. With experience, scorers can become quite consistent and young authors can be sorted into broad groups of proficiency levels. However, the danger with this type of scoring is that it can be highly subjective and generally offers only minimal diagnostic information to inform the course of instruction.

Many writing curricula include their own rubrics for specialized holistic scoring. These rubrics narrow the broad categories so that individual strengths and weaknesses can be identified. The *6+1 Traits of Writing* (written by Ruth Culham and published by Scholastic) method of teaching and assessing writing contains its own rubric, specially designed to view a piece of writing based on ideas, organization, voice, sentence fluency, word choice, and conventions.

The CraftPlus® K-8 Writing Program, published by Maupin House, includes two types of flexible rubrics designed by Marcia Freeman to identify specific *Target Skills* that have been taught during a period of instruction. The teacher selects a skill—or multiple skills—based on current instruction.

The standard of quality remains the same, but the number of skills can range from a single skill to multiple skills being assessed at once within the holistic format. Within the *CraftPlus* framework, the specific writing-craft skills taught are sorted into three categories: organizational, composing, and conventions.

CraftPlus Single-skill Rubric

Target Skills:	**3** Student applies skill competently and creatively.	**2** Student applies skill competently.	**1** Student attempts to apply skill.	**0** Student does not attempt to apply skill.
Target Skill: ____________				

CraftPlus Multiple-skills Rubric

Target Skills:	**3** Student applies skill competently and creatively.	**2** Student applies skill competently.	**1** Student attempts to apply skill.	**0** Student does not attempt to apply skill.
Organizational: ____________ ____________				
Composing: ____________ ____________ ____________				
Conventions: ____________ ____________				

Final score (average): __________

Holistic scoring, while helpful in focusing on the effectiveness of the whole piece, has its limitations. If you are using a rubric to score your students' work, try to objectify your evaluation by identifying skills or traits as in these curricular rubrics. Your scoring will become a composite of the student's strengths and weaknesses, and you can use the information gleaned from your assessment to help you plan for subsequent instruction.

If you are charged with transferring the rubric scores into percentages for grades, you will find that rubrics are not compatible. Consider some of the following classroom-friendly options for evaluating your students' growth and proficiency in writing on an ongoing basis.

Process-based assessment. When assessing complete pieces of writing, we have several choices, including the holistic rubric discussed previously. However, there are times when we want to look beyond the *piece* as a whole and step back to view the *process* as a whole.

Process-based assessment means evaluating each stage of the writing process. The student's final score is derived from his or her proficiency throughout the writing process: pre-writing/planning, drafting, revising, editing, and publishing.

By breaking the writing process into its component parts, we are able to view the student's *process* skills and determine where individual strengths and opportunities for growth exist within that process.

Some students are very skilled at pre-writing and planning but begin to lose their steam when actually writing a rough draft. Others may rush past the planning stage and jump into their writing, leading to a disorganized draft lacking in focus. Some students may have strong drafts but stall out when it comes to making improvements via revision and editing.

When using a process-based assessment, we can determine at which point of the process a student may need intervention or assistance:

	Needs improvement	**Meets expectations**	**Exceeds expectations**
Pre-writing/ planning			
Drafting			
Revising			
Editing			
Publishing			

Of course, process-based assessments can only be used when students are working on complete pieces over an extended period of time. Realistically, we know that every piece will not be taken through the entire writing process. However, when planning pieces that will be taken to the publishing stage, be sure to teach and model each stage of the writing process so that students are well-acquainted with your expectations.

Mini-assessments. If your instruction is built upon writing-craft skills, you will want to see if your students can apply those skills in isolation before asking them to apply multiple skills in a genre piece. This is when mini-assessments are handy tools. You can assess the "skill of the week" before moving on to new skills.

For instance, if you have been teaching strong verbs during the week, by Friday you can ask students to write a brief paragraph describing an action-oriented picture using at least five strong verbs. During a week when you have been studying alliteration, you might ask students to write a short alliterative tongue twister to demonstrate the skill.

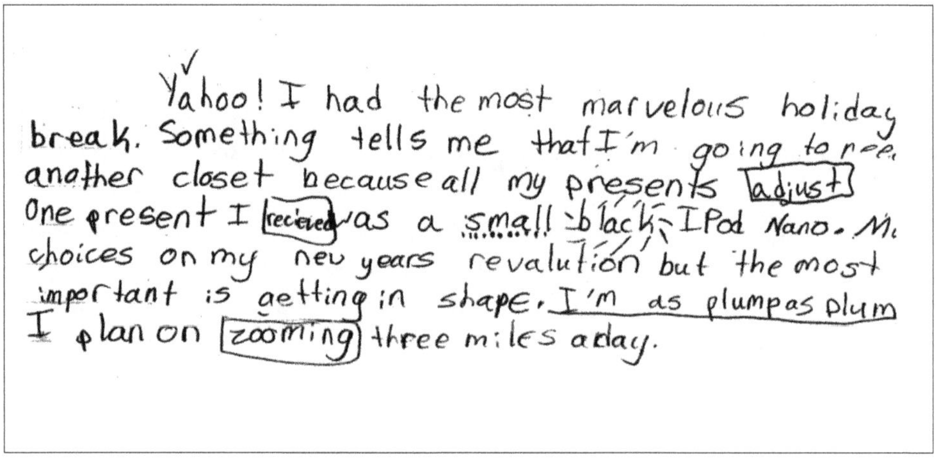
Yahoo! I had the most marvelous holiday break. Something tells me that I'm going to nee another closet because all my presents adjust! One present I recieved was a small black IPod Nano. M choices on my new years revalution but the most important is getting in shape. I'm as plump as plum I plan on zooming three miles a day.

MINI-ASSESSMENT PARAGRAPH:
Use exclamation as a beginning technique; draw a box around three strong verbs; draw a sunburst around descriptive attributes; underline a simile – Brynn, fifth grade

Mini-assessments are very efficient in determining students' proficiency with language conventions at all levels. Primary students can be assigned the quick task of writing one complete sentence using a capital letter at the beginning of the sentence, spaces between the words, and an appropriate end mark at the end of the sentence.

Intermediate students might be assigned the task of writing one line of dialogue with correct punctuation. Mature writers may be given a more challenging task, like writing a brief description of a character containing one simile, one metaphor, and two strong verbs:

> *Mrs. Harman sauntered into the room like a strutting peacock. Her face gleamed with a mix of triumph and satisfaction. Even if it was for just one day, she was the queen bee in our neighborhood hive.*

Use mini-assessments in between the assignment of lengthier pieces. Continually monitor the progress of your students as they acquire new skills. Then, when you know they have mastered each skill in isolation, you will be ready for them to apply multiple skills in a complete piece.

Based upon your design of the mini-assessment and your plan to use the data, you can employ a simple "yes/no" evaluation or single-skill rubric, or you may find a weighted checklist to be of value.

Weighted checklist. I have tried many ways to derive a percentage as a writing grade. One attempt was to assign a numeric value to each craft skill applied. For instance, when five strong verbs are required in a brief descriptive mini-assessment, why not assign each strong verb the value of twenty points?

The problem I quickly discovered is that it was too easy to sink a child's grade. For instance, a child who only applied three strong verbs was receiving a grade of sixty percent when the piece was beautifully written and quite effective. Other students may have written incomplete pieces but had slapped down five strong verbs in a list, qualifying them for 100 percent. There was too big of a discrepancy between scores. Overall, this system did not accurately represent my students' writing proficiency.

So, I developed a weighted checklist that has worked well for me and has been much more accurate in representing the quality of my students' writing. I first assign sixty percent to the complete piece; if you finish the assignment and turn it in on time, you can't fail. Next, I assign numeric values to the specific required skills. This way, I am building on the complete piece of writing and evaluating craft as the "icing on the cake."

Weighted Checklist for a Brief Edited Piece

Writing - Weighted Checklist - Four Required Skills

Assignment complete	(60%)	_____
Five strong verbs	(10%)	_____
One simile	(10%)	_____
Spelling	(10%)	_____
Capitalization and punctuation	(10%)	_____

Weighted Checklist for an Unedited Fictional Narrative

Writing - Weighted Checklist - Eight Required Skills

Assignment complete	(60%)	_____
Beginning technique	(5%)	_____
Time and place transitions	(5%)	_____
Logical sequence of events	(5%)	_____
At least five strong verbs	(5%)	_____
Development of the main character	(5%)	_____
Description of the setting	(5%)	_____
Development of the plot	(5%)	_____
Ending technique	(5%)	_____

As you can see, weighted checklists are designed by the teacher to evaluate the specific skills being taught during a unit of writing instruction. (See the templates in the **Appendix** to create your own weighted checklists.) However, the completion of the piece is of supreme value, allowing students to build their grades by infusing the piece with the required writing-craft skills and language conventions.

Portfolio assessment. Portfolio assessment is regaining some popularity, and rightly so. Just the word *portfolio* carries the connotation of the artist at work. When students assemble their writing in portfolios, to be scrutinized as a body of work, they become *authors*.

Using portfolio assessment, of course, goes far beyond the simple act of collecting pieces of writing. You must decide exactly how you will score these pieces to produces grades representative of your students' work.

Most teachers who use portfolio assessment agree that the contents required for inclusion must be determined in advance and deadlines should be set to ensure that students remain productive over the prescribed period of time.

When planning the genres you will cover in a marking period, determine a realistic number of pieces to be completed, representative of the genres taught (e.g., *By the end of the marking period, your portfolio should contain the following published pieces: four poems, one fictional narrative, and one friendly letter.*). Each marking period, the contents of the portfolio expand with the breadth of your students' work.

Criteria for portfolio contents should be clearly stated in advance so that students know the expectations. Throughout the marking period, conduct daily writers' workshop activities, providing mini-lessons, daily writing time, and ample opportunities for peer and instructor feedback.

It would be impractical and overwhelming to wait until the end of the marking period to evaluate all students' portfolio contents. Grade pieces as you go along, providing substantive feedback. Many teachers who use portfolio assessments consider pieces to be works in progress, allowing students to revise pieces based on teacher feedback and improve their grades.

Author and educator Laurie S. Bottoms, in discussing her evolving use of portfolios in the classroom, admits that her first attempts did not yield significant progress for her students. As she continued to reflect and refine her practice, she discovered the value of giving ownership over the writing process to her students. She made feedback central to the revision process, and after completing publishing activities that were labor intensive for the teacher, she decided one year to turn the job of publishing over to her students:

> *Their creativity produced far more satisfying forms of publication than I had imagined. For instance, one class held an informal evening "Coffee House" of readings for the class and friends; one class invited parents and friends to a more formal reading of their work in the library; one class took a thematic approach, posting up writing in the form of "Letters on War and Peace"; one class simply photocopied the best piece chosen from each portfolio.*
>
> **— Laurie S. Bottoms, "Notes on the Portfolio Approach to Teaching Writing, "*Quarterly of the National Writing Project and the Center for the Study of Writing and Literacy***

For the writing classroom, portfolios can provide a conduit to ownership for your students. They can begin to view themselves as authors collecting a body of work. They can grow in their ability to be reflective, self-evaluative, critical thinkers. Portfolios offer the opportunity for you and your students to view the development of their writing proficiency over the course of the school year through authentic compositions taken through the complete writing process.

Standardized assessments. We discussed standardized assessments at length in the first chapter. When assessing writing—no matter how finely trained and consistent the scorers claim to be—there will always be an element of subjectivity. There will also be a format that is not consistent with your regular classroom writing workshop.

In the ideal writing classroom, students are able to discuss ideas, receive feedback, and use classroom resources. They are generally not required to write a complete piece within a prescribed number of minutes. Their writing is assessed by the tools you have chosen, and they are probably self-selecting topics rather than responding to prompts. Additionally, they usually have an authentic sense of purpose and audience.

It would be unwise to abandon that meaningful authenticity to spend the year mimicking the test format. Instead, implement the structure of writing workshop in your classroom throughout the year, support students through the writing process, and give them choices in topic and approach. Supply a viable purpose and audience for their writing projects. Make it your first priority to develop authors; then, you can introduce your students to the testing environment in the weeks preceding the assessment.

About a month before the assessment, begin to introduce the constraints and requirements of the assessment. If your students must discern the mode of the prompt and respond accordingly, practice reading prompts and determining mode. If your students are given one specific genre in the assessment, then review the structure and craft of that genre. If they will be required to write within a prescribed number of minutes, then have them practice writing a complete piece within that time frame.

When students have practiced by writing a practice piece in a prescribed amount of time in response to a given prompt, allow them to evaluate their own pieces with the rubric that will be used by scorers of the standardized assessment. Ask them to identify what they've done well and where they can make improvements. Then, practice one more time.

I have found that two practice writings—allowing students to self-assess their writing and receive feedback in between—are very effective in preparing them for a standardized writing assessment. One practice does not allow them to apply the goals they have set through self-assessment and feedback; more than two practices can lead to burnout and rehearsed formulaic responses.

Some states, in addition to standardized assessment of written compositions, administer a multiple-choice writing test. While this type of test does not evaluate a student's proficiency or effectiveness as a writer, it does determine whether or not a student has knowledge of writing terminology and is able to identify writing-craft skills that are applied in written samples.

These types of assessments can be useful in the classroom from time to time to monitor student progress in the acquisition of knowledge *about* writing in addition to the practice *of* writing. If a student's work lacks organization or the student consistently misapplies a craft skill, perhaps the student lacks a clear understanding of planning or has incorrectly identified the craft skill. Multiple-choice assessments can be helpful in determining your students' knowledge of the terminology, patterns, and practices associated with good writing. They are also objective measures.

No matter which type of standardized assessment your state implements, you have a responsibility to prepare your students for the format of the assessment. Learn about the demands of your state's assessments and prepare accordingly. This does NOT mean that the entire year should be spent teaching to the format of the test. Rather, teach writing *well* all year long, and when the test is approaching, familiarize your students with the demands of the format and its scoring system.

Chapter Three
The Writing Workshop

"I only write when I am inspired. Fortunately, I am inspired at 9 o'clock every morning."

—William Faulkner

A Time for Writing

There are many choices to make when structuring your writing workshop, but there is one absolute principle to which you must adhere: *students must write every day.* When learning to play a musical instrument, young musicians will show little or no improvement in their musical proficiency if their only playing time is during the weekly lesson. The concept is the same for any skill we seek to acquire, whether music, sports, or academics. Without daily practice, optimum development will not occur.

During daily writing workshop, you will be teaching a brief mini-lesson and your students will be given time to write. Your lesson structures will vary from day to day. Sometimes your students will write individually and sometimes they will write during paired or interactive activities. (If possible, it's often motivational to set aside additional time for daily self-selected free writing.)

Look carefully at your schedule and designate a daily, consistent block of time—thirty to forty-five minutes—as your daily writing block. Be consistent with the schedule and procedures related to this writing block. Let your daily writing procedure become a routine, predictable part of each school day. While the format and content of instruction will vary, your students will gain a level of comfort when they can rely on a daily time for writing.

What Does the Daily Writing Workshop Look Like?

A large portion of the time devoted to writing instruction and practice should, of course, be spent *writing.* Students should be creating brief pieces to practice the application of skills or should be working on longer pieces that they intend to complete and take through the stages of the writing process.

Ideally, the daily writing block should be divided into segments: a brief and concise mini-lesson, time for writing practice and application, and time to share and reinforce the skills taught during workshop. Generally, you should devote about ten to fifteen minutes to each segment of the writing workshop.

The Daily Writing Workshop: Initial Lessons

Focused Mini-lesson	10-15 minutes	• Introduce skills. • Provide teacher models. • Share literature models. • Create interactive models. • Review and refine skills.
Dedicated Writing Time	10-15 minutes	• Students apply skills in pairs or small groups. • Students apply skills in brief practice pieces. • Students apply skills by revising previously written pieces. • The teacher circulates, assists, and clarifies misconceptions.
Share Writing and Reinforce Skills	10-15 minutes	• Volunteers share their work. • The teacher selects student models to share. • Students participate in peer conferences. • Students participate in small-group conferences.

As your students gain proficiency with skills, you will continue to review and revisit them, but your pattern will begin to change slightly. At this point, you can use student models (only in a positive manner), continue to use literature models, and shorten the length of the mini-lesson, giving the students more time to apply the skill in a meaningful context.

After teaching a cluster of several related skills, assign a full piece of writing that will be taken through the stages of the writing process. Require that all skills taught during the cluster of mini-lessons be applied in this piece. For these application pieces, instructional time should be reduced and writing time should be increased as students work through the stages of the writing process to develop published pieces.

When students are working to publish a comprehensive piece, mini-lessons might only be five minutes in length. Students do not need as much instruction at this point; they need uninterrupted time to write. Brief mini-lessons should focus on skills pulled directly from the students' writing. You may find that you need to re-teach and refine craft skills taught during previous mini-lessons, or you may need to revisit a language convention taught earlier in the year.

The Daily Writing Workshop: Reinforcement Lessons

Focused Mini-lesson	5-10 minutes	• Review required skills. • Briefly share literature models. • Share student models. • Review assignment criteria.
Dedicated Writing Practice	20-25 minutes	• Students write. • The teacher circulates and assists.
Response	5-10 minutes	• Volunteers share brief excerpts. • The teacher shares pre-selected excerpts from student writing (only positive models). • The teacher clarifies misconceptions.

Step One: The Mini-Lesson (Ten-Fifteen Minutes)

Before school begins, determine the writing skills you intend to cover during the year and organize a long-range plan. Consider your academic calendar, and group skills to facilitate genre instruction and content-area integration. (A planning template and a sample long-range plan are included in the **Appendix** for your convenience.)

For instance, if you will be teaching a unit on habitats or geographical landforms, you might want to teach descriptive writing skills at the same time so that students can write detailed descriptions of various habitats or landforms. If you typically require students to research historical figures during Black History Month, plan to teach informational expository skills in February and have students research and write about selected historical figures.

Mark skills on a calendar, but be flexible—knowing that the time allotted for some skills may need to be extended, while instruction of other skills can be accelerated. Once you have selected your skills and created a long-range plan, you are ready to begin teaching targeted mini-lessons that will build your students' writing proficiency in a systematic fashion.

The mini-lesson is the first segment of your daily writing schedule and should consume only ten to fifteen minutes of your writing workshop. During introductory skill lessons, identify and define the skill, model the skill as it is applied in literature, provide teacher models, and work with students to generate examples of the skill.

Literature models, often called *mentor texts*, are essential to building the concept of new skills. Show students how an accomplished author has applied the skill. These models are well crafted, authentic, and readily at hand in the classroom.

From the classroom...

Mini-lesson: strong verbs, grades one-three

Three-five minutes: *The writing-craft skill I am teaching is strong verbs. I begin my lesson by quickly reviewing action verbs with my students. I ask, "What is the action verb in this sentence? I ran to the bus stop." I practice two or three more verbal examples until I am sure students can identify action verbs.*

Three-five minutes: *Next, I tell them that some action verbs are considered "strong verbs" because they are very precise and easy for the reader to picture. I provide examples and non-examples. "He* ***went*** *outside. This sentence contains the verb 'went,' but I can't picture 'went' very easily. He* ***walked*** *outside is stronger. He* ***crawled*** *outside"." I ask the students for a few more examples and list them on the board.*

Five minutes: *I take out the book* **The Wind Blew** *by Pat Hutchins. I tell students that I will begin reading the book, and when they hear a strong verb they should raise their hands. I read the book. Each time students raise their hands, I stop and ask them to identify the strong verb. I may select one of my high-functioning writers to continue recording strong verbs on the board as we identify them. Once I feel confident that students understand the concept, I can stop reading and move on to the workshop part of the lesson.*

After a skill has been introduced, you will build understanding and begin to bring the skill closer to the students by generating your own examples and having students offer suggestions. This interactive practice begins to turn over ownership of the skill to your students. As students practice and gain fluency with the skill, you will build a repertoire of student models to share as well.

Cluster skills so that after students have practiced each skill in isolation, they can easily apply them together in one larger piece. For example, if you are working on a poetry unit, you may want to teach individual mini-lessons on rhythm, rhyme, and similes. Students can practice these skills in isolation as you are teaching them, and then apply them collectively in a single poem or a collection of poetry.

Step Two: Writing Practice (Ten-Fifteen Minutes)

After the mini-lesson, students should be given an uninterrupted block of time to write or otherwise practice their facility with the new writing-craft skill. Most often, writing during workshop should be an individual endeavor, but sometimes it will be a partner or small-group activity. These shared writing experiences are most effective when skills are new, and many students may need support in order to understand and apply the skill.

When focused on an individual skill, writing practice should be brief, isolating the skill in a concise sample. You may ask students to make a list of examples or write a two- to three-sentence piece applying the new skill. After you have taught several related skills, students will be ready to apply them in a lengthier work that stretches over several days.

When any skill is introduced, there will be students who catch on immediately, students who achieve only a shallow and tenuous understanding of the skill, and probably those who have not effectively processed the new information at all. For this reason, it's important to pair students or allow them to work in small groups when applying new skills.

When pairing students, it is generally best to avoid matching students with others of the same achievement level. Try to make low-to-middle and middle-to-high pairings. This strategy helps ensure optimum peer-assisted learning for both partners.

Small cooperative groups, containing three to four students each, can also be an effective way to scaffold and support learners of a new skill. Set clear expectations for groups and role-play interactions ahead of time. Assign responsibilities within groups and demonstrate examples and non-examples of give-and-take behaviors in conversation.

On the second or third day you are teaching a skill—or when you determine that everyone has an understanding of the skill—students should be working individually. Provide an assignment, generate a few examples, answer questions, and then let students write.

My daughter once complained to me that she became agitated when teachers gave a writing assignment and then continually offered additional pointers and reminders as students were working. I shared her annoyance at these teachers who just wouldn't stop talking but soon found that I was one of them. Remembering my daughter's words improved my practice. I learned to be quiet and allow my students to write.

From the classroom...

Ten-fifteen minutes: *After our strong-verb mini-lesson, I give directions for writing workshop. Students will work in pairs since the skill is new. Each pair receives a picture prompt. When they look at their picture prompt, each pair must list five strong verbs that indicate the action taking place in the picture. Then they are to write two to three sentences containing these strong verbs. Students should read over their work, underlining their strong verbs and making sure their sentences make sense and their verbs identify specific actions that can be easily pictured by the reader.*

Your role during this writing practice time is to circulate and observe. Mentally gather data or keep anecdotal records to help you monitor the strengths, weaknesses, and ongoing milestones of individual writers in your classroom. Since this is a practice and not an assessment, assist students if they are confused. Clarify misconceptions, redirect students as needed, and ask leading questions if necessary to elicit the desired skill.

While you are not interrupting the entire class, you can kneel at the sides of some reluctant or struggling writers to offer assistance and help them organize their thoughts. Your writing workshop can become a time of differentiated instruction and targeted intervention as you rove and assist students in a meaningful, authentic venue. While the topic of intervention is a book unto itself, I have provided a quick, on-the-spot intervention guide in the **Appendix**. Use this guide to assist your students in getting beyond common writing roadblocks.

Step Three: Response (Ten-Fifteen Minutes)

Before the end of each daily writing workshop, set aside time to share student writing and reinforce the skills and concepts you are teaching. This response time will allow students to showcase their writing and receive feedback from others. Of course, doing so requires vulnerability on the part of students and should be handled with advance preparation and well-understood guidelines.

Response time can be conducted in a variety of formats. When skills are new, you may want to pre-select students who have demonstrated a solid understanding of the concept. Ask these students to read their brief practice pieces to the class and, after each reading, be very specific in identifying the application of the new skill. These student models are valuable teaching tools for fledgling writers.

As students gain competence with the skill, ask volunteers to share their practice pieces. If you have established an encouraging, respectful classroom environment, students will be comfortable sharing their work with the class. Be very specific in your praise, affirming application of the desired skill. Teach and expect students to respond to writing in a way that is positive and constructive.

From the classroom...

I call on pairs one at a time, asking one partner to read the strong verbs the pair has underlined, and asking the other partner to read the description. I praise the use of strong verbs and point out my favorite strong verb each pair shares. At the end of response time, I carefully address misconceptions I have noticed without singling out or embarrassing anyone. If misconceptions cannot be clarified easily, I will address them with the whole class during a subsequent mini-lesson.

Sometimes you will want to have students conduct peer conferences during response. If you pair students for peer conferences, teach and role-model the expected behaviors. During peer conferences, the young writer sharing his or her piece deserves respect from the listener. Role-play examples and non-examples of active listening behaviors, specific praise, and appropriate questioning techniques.

Small-group conferences can serve as mini-author's-chair sessions, in which students share their work with three or four others who offer specific praise and ask clarifying questions. Be sure to budget enough response time so that each student has the opportunity to share his or her work.

When students have taken a piece through the entire writing process, they deserve an audience. In many classrooms, a special seat is designated as the author's chair. Students sit in this chair as they make their work public, reading it before a live audience. If time permits, listeners can offer specific praise or ask clarifying questions.

In other classrooms, students stand in front of the class to read their pieces. In this setting, it's generally best to allow students to practice their presentation skills—engaging their listeners with physical gestures and vocal inflections, monitoring volume, enunciating words clearly, and making occasional eye contact.

By conducting daily response and regular sharing of published works, you will accomplish more than reinforcing writing-craft skills and helping students articulate their thoughts about writing. An invaluable benefit for your students is the sense of community you will establish as students communicate author to author.

Auxiliary Activities

While writing workshop is the focal point of daily writing instruction and practice, auxiliary writing activities can enhance learning and motivation. Reading integration activities are very valuable for teachers who feel pressed for time and need to reinforce writing skills within the context of the reading block.

If you have time to add them to your day, writing warm-ups and free-writing are valuable add-ons to your instruction. Daily writing warm-ups are quick eye-openers to review writing-craft skills. Free-writing is a journaling activity with self-selected topics and formats.

Reading Integration Activities

Many teachers teach reading during a daily uninterrupted reading block of ninety minutes or more and are not permitted to teach writing during this time. While the legislative focus on reading is well-intended, the isolation of this one language process may be counterproductive.

By using your reading texts to reinforce writing skills, you can promote re-reading, critical thinking, and higher-level comprehension of the reading text. You won't be *teaching* writing during the reading block, but your students will be actively associating writing and reading. Your students will learn to read with the writer's eye.

Reading integration activities can be used as workstation tasks, homework assignments, or independent work following a reading selection. These literature-based writing activities can be paired with any narrative story from your reading series and used multiple times with different stories for skill review. Here's an example of a reading integration activity:

Writing: Time and Place Transitions	**Reading:** Sequence of Events
Skim the story and jot down the time and place transitions you find in the order they are used in the story. Consider how each time or place transition was used to advance the plot and help the reader create a timeline of events.	

You can design your own reading integration activities or use the ones provided in the **Appendix**. Your immediate objective is to review a writing skill while reinforcing reading comprehension; however, your broader goal is to integrate language processes in a way that makes learning meaningful.

Writing Warm-ups

If your class has difficulty transitioning into your writing lessons, a brief writing warm-up will be helpful. This warm-up should be posted on the board at the beginning of your writing workshop. If you are teaching in a departmentalized situation, warm-ups can be particularly useful in getting your students quickly focused as they enter the classroom.

A writing warm-up should be a direct statement that begins with a verb and should provide a clear, craft-based objective. The warm-up should focus on the writing-craft skill you will be teaching during your mini-lesson (unless you choose to review a skill for reinforcement). If the skill is new, you may want to include an example of a desired response.

The point of a writing warm-up is to transition your students into thinking as writers. Warm-ups are a springboard for a successful writing workshop. Even if the skill is new and students are unsure, the thinking they do to try to meet the objective will stretch their minds and build a conceptual foundation for learning.

A typical writing warm-up looks like this:

Personification

Complete the chart to give human actions and qualities to non-human entities. The first one is done for you as an example.

Non-human entity	**Action verb**	**Attitude**
rain	*dancing*	*joyful*
wind		
clouds		
tree		
car		

Choose one non-human entity and write a sentence using personification.

Example: The joyful rain danced on the sidewalk.

On subsequent days, you can offer a warm-up activity that asks students to return to the original activity and apply the skill in a poetic description:

PERSONIFICATION - KELLY, FIFTH GRADE

Writing warm-ups should require only a few minutes to complete. As students are finishing the task, ask volunteers to share their responses. Students unsure of the objective can learn from the modeling of others. After the writing warm-up, you may even want to use these responses in your mini-lesson and have students use them to build a brief piece of writing during workshop.

Free-writing

I learned from my students that daily, self-selected "free-writing" is highly motivational and leads young writers to develop their own voices and directions. Time can be set aside on a regular basis, or free-writing can be encouraged when students complete required assignments.

Free-writing should be a risk-free-writing time. It's not a time to make assignments or present writing prompts. However, be sure to define parameters so that students know they will not be writing anything inappropriate or hurtful to another student. Beyond that, let them write!

A great idea is to set aside at least ten minutes at the beginning of your writing block for students to just write freely in their journals. Opening a writing workshop with this activity will provide a smooth transition into writing. It will also "prime the pump" and get your students' creative juices flowing.

Circulate during this time and converse with students informally. These impromptu discussions provide unplanned opportunities for growth and learning—random, teachable moments of great meaning and value.

Some of your students will jump into their writing with great focus and enthusiasm. Others will encounter difficulties. Use the following troubleshooting guide to keep everyone on task and make the most of your daily free-writing time:

Free-writing Troubleshooting Guide

When students are stuck and can't think of what to write:

- *Encourage them to make a list of the things they enjoy doing.*
- *Have them list people and places that can become characters and settings.*
- *Suggest that they make a list of topics they know a lot about.*
- *Point out a classroom object or area and have them write to describe it.*
- *Direct them to write about the things that have happened since they walked into your classroom.*

When students say they have finished writing:

- *Ask if they would like to conference with you and revise this piece for classroom publication.*
- *Suggest that they re-read for specific writing-craft skills that have been a focus of reading lessons. For example, suggest that they go back and look for descriptive attributes relating to character or setting; point out a place where they can add clues for inference rather than making a direct statement; have the student identify overuse of the word "then" and replace it with appropriate transitions.*
- *Challenge students to try out a new genre, like writing a skit or a comic book.*

When students are reluctant to share their free-writing with you:

- *Respect their privacy and build trust. Trust is the basis of your relationship with your students and is the foundation on which discipline is built.*
- *Tell them you don't have to read their free-writing pieces, but you would like to know the topic and genre. This will help you maintain control of the free-writing environment without stifling students.*
- *Ask them to identify a classmate with whom they would like to share their work.*
- *Work with them to set a date when they will share their writing with you.*
- *Share your own writing with them to build a sense of community and shared experience.*

When students want to draw during free-writing time:

- *Drawing can often serve as a catalyst for writing. Give students a time limit for sketching, after which point they should begin writing about the picture. Help younger students create a word bank associated with the picture.*
- *Students who enjoy drawing may enjoy creating cartoons. Have students sketch cartoon boxes and write text in speech bubbles. After revising and editing, students can publish cartoons on folded strips of paper.*
- *Challenge students to create a rebus story.*
- *Write a poem about one of their drawings to model a possible written response.*

When students don't want to stop free-writing to move on to your mini-lesson:

- *Even though it is difficult to stop a student from writing, you must reconvene your class for the mini-lesson. Encourage students to jot down five or fewer words to serve as memory triggers when they return to the piece.*
- *Allow students to take their free-writing journals home to continue writing, with the assurance that they will return the journals to school the following day.*
- *If you are having this problem with several students, you may want to collect journals at the end of free-writing time and keep them in a box or on a shelf. Allow students to have access to journals at other points during the day if they finish assignments early.*

If you are able to implement free-writing in your classroom, be sure to specify procedures, expectations, and a discrete time limit for this activity. You will find that students train themselves to adapt to the limitations you set and employ without exception.

Many students take great pride in the pieces they create in their free-writing journals. A few times during the year, allow students to self-select a piece from their journals for publication. Over the course of a week, you might even be able to integrate your writing workshop with these self-selected projects as you help students revise, edit, and bring their creative pieces to the publication stage.

Materials: Writer's Notebook and Teacher's Notebook

With many curriculum areas, you need to purchase a wealth of instructional materials. Because writing comes from the individual, there is no need for prefabricated workbooks or volumes of information. Writing is real and authentic. It comes from and belongs to your students. Therefore, the supplies you will need are raw materials that your students will use to create their own texts.

Writer's Notebook

The centerpiece of your writing workshop should be the writer's notebooks. All writers need a place to keep their work organized, store their ideas, and house their resources in an easily accessible manner.

Writer's notebooks are low cost and simple to create. Give each student a three-ring binder, paper, and tabbed dividers. You can create your own names for each section of the notebook, but the core sections should be:

- Resources
- Practice Pieces
- Assessment Pieces
- Published Pieces or Portfolio

The "Resources" section of your writer's notebooks will be empty at the beginning of the year. As you teach skills and create or reproduce models, lists, and examples, this section will house those resources. This dynamic section of the writer's notebook grows as new skills are learned, and it should be actively used as students are writing.

The "Practice Pieces" section will be the most frequently used portion of the notebook. This is where students will turn each day when they are required to apply the skill you have taught and demonstrated during the mini-lesson. Through brief practice pieces, students apply skills to work toward mastery as they develop their own collection of writing-craft samples.

Assessment pieces can be stored in the notebook as a tangible record of student progress. If you require students to review their assessment pieces and make corrections and revisions, these pieces become valuable learning tools and empower students to grow as writers.

Published pieces can be collected in the back of the writer's notebook. As pieces are added over the course of the year, this section of the notebook forms a chronological record of each student's writing growth. If you prefer to protect published pieces by keeping them in a separate location, you can store them in portfolios. At the end of the year, give the portfolios to your students and let them review their own development as writers.

Aside from these core sections of the writer's notebook, you may want to develop one or two other sections to meet the needs of your students. Optional sections may include:

- Free Writing
- Spelling
- Grammar, Usage, and Mechanics
- Ideas

At the end of the school year, each writer's notebook will be the textbook that was developed gradually and authentically throughout the course of your instruction. Students will have resources and models ready to use in future writing endeavors, as well as a keepsake collection of personal compositions.

Teacher's Notebook

The teacher's notebook grows and becomes, throughout the year, much like the students' notebooks. During your first year of implementing a writer's workshop approach, you will be creating, gathering, learning, and collecting. Your notebook will give you a place to organize the tangible results of your efforts and make them accessible in subsequent years.

Your notebook should be a three-ring binder with dividers to organize instructional materials. It may look like the notebooks belonging to your students, but the contents and purpose will differ. Tabbed dividers in your teacher's notebook should include:

- Lesson Plans
- Templates and Reproducibles
- Student Models
- Literature Models (lists, notes)

The purpose of the "Lesson Plans" section of your notebook is obvious. You work to create lesson plans each year, and by saving them in your notebook, you will decrease your work load in subsequent years. You will create a customized teacher's manual to guide you through writing instruction.

Of course, this teacher's manual will be fluid and dynamic. As you revise and refine your lessons, make notes and changes. You will probably find it necessary to add, combine, or delete lessons. Make notes after lessons to help you remember unexpected outcomes, misconceptions, and strategies that worked well.

Your notebook will increase your efficiency by making templates and reproducibles easily accessible. As you create or locate resources like graphic organizers, lists of writing-craft examples, or grammar tips, save a copy in the "Templates and Reproducibles" section of your notebook.

Keep lists of literature models or jot down passages that you use to demonstrate writing-craft skills. Often, the most effective resources are those that come from classroom experience. For example, if your students have searched literature models to find examples of strong verbs, compile the examples they have located and make copies for student notebooks. Save copies of student models and use them in subsequent years to demonstrate high-quality written responses for various assignments.

Your teacher's notebook may seem like a task to create, but it will be an invaluable resource as years continue. While publishers' teacher guides can be very comprehensive manuals, your notebook will be relevant and authentic, just like your students' writing.

Management: Peer Conferences, Behavior, and Time

Your three main areas of management during a writing workshop are peer interactions, on-task behavior, and time management. Despite your best intentions and thorough preparedness, a weakness in one of these elements of management can cause your writing workshop to be ineffective, your classroom environment to be unproductive, and the attitudes of the students and the teacher to turn negative.

Peer Interactions

Throughout your writing workshop, students should be encouraged to respond to writing. This situation makes your young authors vulnerable, and the wrong kinds of interactions can ruin your writing community.

Some teachers tell students to offer two compliments and one suggestion during a peer conference. Others teach students to provide specific praise, naming the craft skills evident in the peer's writing. If a rubric is being used to score a piece of writing, it is often helpful to let the rubric guide the peer interactions.

Marcia Freeman, in *Building a Writing Community* (Maupin House, 2003), discusses "knee-to-knee conferences," a specific format for peer conferences used in the CraftPlus K-8 Writing Program. The purpose of knee-to-knee conferences is to identify and positively reinforce the application of a skill being taught and practiced.

Young authors are paired and take turns reading their pieces to each other. The first partner reads his or her piece twice. During the first reading, the listener is quiet while the piece is read in its entirety. After the first reading, the listener makes a personal connection to the text.

During the second reading, the listener stops the reader each time the desired craft skill is heard. For each incidence of the desired craft skill, the listener provides a "did-it-dot," a small round sticker that serves as a tangible reward for applying the craft skill. This conference model is most effective when used with practice pieces that should exhibit the application of a specific craft skill.

Whatever format you use, teach students to speak to each other as supportive peers, using non-threatening, constructive language. Role-play these interactions before putting students in peer conferencing situations. Provide examples and non-examples of acceptable conferencing behaviors. Set structural limitations for conferencing responses.

I have found it helpful to teach students "four Cs" for constructive peer conferences:

- **Connect** to the text: *I have a dog, too, but my dog is a lot lazier than your dog.*
- **Compliment** the author: *You are really good at describing settings. I felt like I was really there!*
- **Critique** the piece by asking a question and/or offering a suggestion: *I could picture your dog's actions, but I couldn't get a clear picture of what he looks like. What does he look like? How would you describe his color and size?*
- **Compliment the craft**: *You used some really great strong verbs, like* tumbled *and* cavorted.

If you teach students a routine for addressing these four points of peer conferencing, their interactions will begin to become second nature. They will automatically connect to text (an integral active reading strategy), encourage each other as authors, offer substantive feedback, and provide specific praise.

You may find it helpful to distribute peer conferencing "sentence starters" as student resources. These kinds of guides give students some concrete assistance in beginning a constructive conference, and they help reduce miscommunication because students are taught to "speak a common language." (See suggestions in "The Four Cs of Peer Conferencing" in the **Appendix**.)

From the classroom...

Ryan, a first-grade student, reads his descriptive poem to me:

Reptile is a ninja of fire.
He throws fire from his hands.
He is green with a black mouth.
He fights at night.

I compliment his description and tell him I find the subject to be original and exciting. I like the way his sentences are complete, all related to the topic, and all begin with capital letters and end with periods. He tells me he has a reptile action figure.

Next, I tell him that I can see these related sentences developing into a descriptive poem. I remind him of the color words and color comparisons we have discussed in recent lessons. I ask him to be more specific with colors.

After sharing his writing with me, Ryan shares it with a peer. Erich listens attentively and connects to the text by telling Ryan that he knows about the action figure. Then, Erich asks a question that prompts a revision. We have recently studied moon phases. Erich asks, "When he's fighting at night, what phase is the moon in?" Ryan seizes upon this question and immediately replies, "It's a crescent moon!"

After revising, taking into consideration my suggestions and Erich's, Ryan's poem looks like this:

Reptile

by Ryan

Reptile is a ninja of fire.
He throws fire
From his gloved hands.
He is dark-leaf green
With a night-black mouth.
He fights at night
When there is a cresent moon.

FREE-VERSE DESCRIPTIVE POEM - RYAN, FIRST GRADE

Ryan's piece reached a level of literary quality that surpassed anything he had written previously. He knew that. He was proud of his poem and enjoyed sharing it with others. With his revision, he was able to move the target that he believed he could reach and began to understand that he could reach an even better target.

When practicing the application of specific writing-craft skills, you may find it helpful to provide students with a tangible means of identifying skills. With younger students, small stickers are very appropriate and motivational. Marcia Freeman calls them "did-it-dots." The listener in a peer conference can add a small sticker to the reader's page each time a skill is applied.

With older students, highlighters or gel pens work well to identify writing-craft skills. The listener highlights, underlines, or circles the writing-craft skill each time it is applied. This tangible reward reinforces the skill and makes it easy for you to rove and spot-check mastery as students are conferencing.

On-task Behavior

Your daily routines will facilitate on-task behavior, but you need to be proactive in anticipating and heading off distractions and lack of productivity. One way to do this is to set very clear expectations.

Post the name of the writing-craft skill you are teaching as a visual reminder of the lesson's objective. This will reinforce the skill and help you and your students stay focused on the objective.

When making assignments, be sure they clearly facilitate the lesson's objective. For instance, if your lesson objective was strong verbs, asking students to write a description of a setting might make the objective hard to achieve. Students need to be writing about action if they are to apply this particular objective.

More tailored, precise assignments requiring students to apply strong verbs might require them to write an account of a sporting event, describe a picture of characters involved in action, or explain a process. Clarity of assignments and expectations help to eliminate confusion and facilitate on-task behavior.

As with any lesson, have your instructional materials and literature models prepared in advance. Nothing unravels attention and behavior quite as quickly as waiting while a teacher locates materials. Building and maintaining your teacher's notebook should be a great help in keeping your materials organized and easily accessible.

Keep mini-lessons targeted, brief, and fast paced. After introducing a skill or concept and demonstrating its use in a literature model, quickly involve students in guided or interactive writing. Too much teacher talk can cause students to disengage. Get students involved in generating examples and make learning active.

Time Management

Most days, your instructional time will be divided evenly into the three sections discussed earlier: mini-lesson, writing practice, and response. When introducing a new skill, the mini-lesson might consume a larger portion of your workshop time. When a skill is being reinforced or assessed, the mini-lesson will be very brief, and students will spend a larger portion of their workshop time writing.

Routine and consistency. Adhere to your daily writing schedule as closely as you can. Routine and consistency are the cornerstones of classroom management. If your writing workshop is sporadic or if the schedule changes from day to day, students will lack the comfort of pattern and predictability needed for optimum growth and learning. Daily workshop routines facilitate the classroom management necessary for a productive, risk-free environment.

If you are unable to devote a full thirty to forty-five minutes of instructional time to writing each day, you can still achieve effective consistency in your daily writing routines and procedures by using some creative time-management strategies.

Workstations. One option is to make writing a workstation as part of your hands-on application time. This works particularly well in primary classrooms where one craft skill is usually the focus of the week's lessons. In the workstation model, you can teach writing-craft skills and share models during your daily mini-lesson while building writing practice into a workstation. These writing assignments should require application of the writing-craft skills being taught throughout the week.

While some students work on writing, others can be conducting an experiment as a follow-up application of a science lesson, and another group can be researching a history topic. Response time after workstations can offer an opportunity for all students to report on their workstation activities and reinforce skills learned through hands-on experience.

Homework journals. Another creative option for making the most of limited instructional time is to assign writing practice in homework journals. A brief directive can be printed on labels and placed at the top of a page in the homework journal. Students can achieve writing practice as homework, and the next day's lesson can begin with response and sharing.

As the week progresses, students can revise homework pieces and incorporate additional writing-craft skills as they are taught.

Content-area integration. Effective teachers know the value of integrating content areas and literacy skills. When possible, make writing part of your science and social studies lessons. For example, students can learn to take notes from non-print media, build sound factual foundations into historical fiction, and write procedures and results for science experiments.

You can integrate content areas into your writing time as well. Generic prompts do not usually inspire great writing. However, topics that stimulate prior knowledge can be very engaging. When students gather data to support their writing, they become self-directed learners applying higher-order thinking skills in a meaningful context.

Linking reading and writing. Finally, the reciprocal power of linking reading and writing is undeniable. In addition to using literature to model effective writing practice, you can use it to inspire students to emulate an author's style or to develop a plot line that mirrors that of a piece you are reading.

Reinforce reading skills by having students write to analyze a piece. Teach them to apply literary terminology and analysis skills. Primary students can build comprehension skills through literature response, writing a concise statement of the main idea, sequencing main events in a story, and describing characters and settings. Older students can write to identify author's purpose, analyze themes, and compare characters, authors, or selections.

One cautionary note: when integrating subjects, it is necessary to be thoroughly prepared and narrowly focused. A common downfall of an integrated curriculum is the tendency to overwhelm students with objectives and possibilities so that they are unclear of expectations and do not see the connections you are trying to make.

Always be sure to identify a limited set of objectives and make sure students understand the expectations. Teach and model procedures, and be systematic in the introduction of new skills, concepts, or procedures. Remember that students find comfort in the predictability of routine and consistency.

Publishing Projects

Now that we've established the importance of routine and consistency, let's discuss the exception to the rule. Every so often, after you have taught a collection of skills associated with a genre, you will need to halt instruction and allow students to use their daily workshop time to take a genre piece to completion, applying all of the skills that were taught over weeks of mini-lessons.

As we discussed earlier, a problematic feature of writing instruction in the age of accountability is the tendency to stop each piece at the rough draft stage. If students are to develop as writers, they must take some pieces through the entire writing process, laboring over word choice and revising their pieces, being held accountable for language conventions, and creating a piece in which they are fully invested.

Because this piece should represent an application of the skills taught during the previous weeks, you must set clear and objective expectations for the assignment. While students are developing self-selected topics into original pieces, they should be fully aware, from the beginning, of the criteria on which you will grade these selections.

Tips

Make announcements. I usually reserve a week or two at the end of each grading period and halt instruction so that students can work on developing genre pieces with self-selected topics. At the beginning of each day's workshop, I start with an announcement rather than a mini-lesson. During my announcement, I will review expectations for our workshop time and offer any reminders students might need, based upon my daily observations.

For instance, if I notice that many students are forgetting to describe the physical features of a main character, I will offer a reminder during my announcements and ask children to check their pieces to be sure that description is included. If not, that will be a revision that should be made that day as students are writing.

Announcements also offer the opportunity to keep students on track, reminding them of the expectations you have set. This brief time also offers you the opportunity to read a small selection from a literature model, reminding students how the "masters" of the craft have applied this skill in their writing. At the end of your workshop time, take the opportunity to reinforce the skill. Share from a student model, demonstrating how one of your young authors revised his or her piece to include the very craft skill you discussed during your announcements.

Establish set guidelines and check progress. Because writing is a personal endeavor and every child works at a different rate, be aware that during these publishing projects, your workshop has the potential to quickly spiral out of control. Establish procedures and routines so that students know what to do, and identify timelines for completion and submission of writing projects. Check the status of the class daily, setting individual goals with students and keeping a record of their progress through the process.

Use the room to group students. If your classroom arrangement facilitates grouping, you may find it helpful to have students physically move to places where they can work at different stages of the writing process. Students who are sharing their writing with a peer as a strategy to develop clarity and effectiveness should be able to find a quiet corner for conferencing. Students who are in the editing stage should gather near spelling and grammar resources. Art supplies can be kept in one area where students can move to work on the final aesthetics of publishing.

Offer tasks to students who finish early. Some students will finish before others. Be prepared to provide them with productive opportunities. They can become the listeners during peer conferences, assist with editing, free-write to develop new pieces, or work on developing a new resource for upcoming lessons by scanning literature models in search of specific writing-craft skills.

Remember revision. When working on publishing projects, focus on revision. During practice work, skill application is the goal, and very little revision is performed. We need to teach students to revise by suggesting places for them to apply specific writing-craft skills in larger works.

Revision will be discussed further in the next chapter, but keep in mind that by revising, students always move their own targets. They will settle for less until they realize that more is possible. Once they have moved the target forward, they are more likely to strive for the same level of achievement in future writing.

During publishing projects, select one or two revision goals for each student. Conference with each student individually and set reasonable goals and timelines for revision. Revision conferences are not negative sessions to point out what is wrong with a piece of writing; they are opportunity sessions to point out what is possible.

However, when we identify the specific skills and the places within the piece where they can be added, students have a road map for revision. Always revisit the student after the revision to follow through and make sure the piece was improved as directed. Celebrate the improvement in writing craft by highlighting it, putting a sticker next to it, or sharing it with the class. Focus on the student's success as a writer.

Rather than waiting until a piece is finished, you can do on-the-spot revision conferences as students work. Teach them to continually re-read and revise as they are writing. This is an authentic form of revision and keeps the process from seeming overwhelming.

From the classroom...

Avery, a fifth-grade student, plans his fictional narrative with great enthusiasm. He raises his hand after writing his opening sentence, eager to share the beginning of his story, "The Candy War." I kneel at his side and he reads quietly to me. His story begins:

> ***Once in the land of Choopuka the kids were happy until the kids went crazy and ate candy everywhere they went.***

First, I compliment the young author. The name Choopuka is unique and fun to pronounce. His ideas are original and should appeal to his peer audience.

Next, I identify a target for revision: description. I tell him the reader would have a difficult time forming a mental picture of Choopuka because he hasn't described the setting.

After his revision, I visit his desk again. We celebrate the revision he has made by sharing it with the class:

> ***Once in the land of Choopuka, there were gumdrop roads and chocolate fences around gingerbread houses. Kids lived there happily...until one day kids went crazy and ate candy everywhere they went.***

Identifying specific goals for revision makes the process concrete and manageable for students. When we ask them to improve their pieces, the field of choices is overwhelming and the result is usually little or no meaningful revision.

Points to Remember

To become writers, students must write every day. Be consistent and provide predictable routines in your writing workshop. Explicitly teach students to communicate with each other as writers, offering respect and affirmation as they seek clarity and effectiveness.

To manage an effective writing workshop, teachers must prepare thoroughly, define specific objectives, and create an environment where students understand their expectations, exhibit on-task behavior, and feel safe practicing writing skills.

To learn writing craft, students must be taught. Your daily writing workshop should begin with concise, targeted mini-lessons. Plan ahead and select the skills your students will need. Plan and prepare lessons with clear objectives in mind.

In the next chapter, we will explore the content of the writing workshop. We will unravel well-crafted writing to discover the ingredients and then use those ingredients of well-crafted writing as the foundation of a writing curriculum.

Chapter Four
The Content of Craft

"The writing process is what writers do; writing craft is what writers know."

— Marcia S. Freeman

Building a Curriculum

Because the elements of writing-craft give substance to your writing instruction, you are able to build a curriculum from identifiable skills. You can select your skills, build your scope and sequence, assemble your models, and plan your lessons. Writing-craft skills become your lesson objectives.

Of course, teaching these skills in isolation is not enough to create students who are skilled, effective writers. You will need to organize your curriculum so that after you teach, model, and practice skills in isolation, students can apply them collectively in a complete piece of writing.

For example, a primary teacher may teach beginning capitalization, end punctuation, descriptive attributes for color and shape, and onomatopoeia over a three-week period, and then guide students in applying all of these skills in one descriptive writing piece that is taken through the entire writing process.

An intermediate teacher can teach a beginning technique, strong verbs, sensory words, time-order transitions, and an ending technique over the course of two weeks. Then, during the third week, have students compose a piece of writing that contains the skills you have taught. Your grading will be more objective because you have identifiable skills set as part of your criteria for the assignment.

On the following pages, you will find an annotated glossary of writing-craft skills. Draw from these skills in building your curriculum. Use the mini-lesson workshop format described in **Chapter Two** to design your lessons. Assemble literature models and organize skills so that several skills can be taught in succession and then applied in a complete piece of writing.

Suggested Writing-craft Skills

Definitions, Tips, and Examples

Alliteration – Alliteration is the repetition of a beginning sound.

Lazy Laura was late for lunch.

Alliteration is appropriate to teach at all age levels. It produces an auditory aesthetic that attracts the reader. Alliteration can enhance a theme, establish a rhythm, move the reader quickly along, or create anticipation.

Note: Avoid misconceptions and clearly communicate that alliteration is the repetition of an initial *sound*, not a beginning *letter.* (A common misconception for children is that *circus* and *clown* are alliterative because they begin with the same letter or that *circus* and *serious* are not alliterative because they begin with different letters.)

Asides to the reader – An aside to the reader is a voice technique in which the author digresses from the story to directly address the reader.

Now, dear reader, do not think the story ends here.

Asides are often used in theatre, when the actor's speech is directed toward the audience and is not supposed to be heard by the other actors on stage. Authors of fiction sometimes use asides to introduce a narrator's voice and share opinions or information. A well-crafted aside makes the reader feel privy to "insider" information and thus more involved in the story and connected to the author.

Beginning techniques – Authors try to "hook" readers by beginning a piece in a compelling way. There are many different types of beginning techniques that are commonly applied in both fiction and nonfiction pieces. Some typical beginning techniques follow.

Dialogue

"Can you remember what ol' Sam looked like?" Joshua looked up at me with sadness in his eyes.

Dialogue, when used as a narrative beginning technique, can hook the reader by creating the feeling that the action has already begun and the reader is joining the characters in the middle of a scene. In expository pieces, a line of dialogue can be used as a compelling beginning hook as well. A quotation from someone associated with the topic of the piece can quickly draw the reader's attention. Beginning around second grade, developing writers should be able to use dialogue hooks proficiently.

Exclamation

Eureka! I finally found a way to get my family to reduce waste by recycling.

Writers use exclamations to show excitement or emotion. They sometimes begin a piece with an exclamation, hoping that the reader will get excited, too, and want to read on.

Exclamations as beginning techniques can be used in both narrative and expository pieces and can be used proficiently by primary and intermediate writers.

Idiom

Birds of a feather flock together.

Idioms are figures of speech that act as language shortcuts and are often metaphoric in nature. When used as a beginning technique, idioms can give the reader a tacit understanding and the feeling of being a language "insider." Idioms are most effectively taught to mature writers in late elementary years and beyond.

Introduction of the main character

Sam Johnson was an eight-year-old magician.

A story or an expository piece can start with a description of the essential or predominant traits of the most important character or person in the piece. Students of all ages are very familiar with this technique in fictional narratives and biographies, and developing writers are usually ready for this technique by late first to early second grade.

Onomatopoeia

***Thwack**! My eyes were closed when the bat finally connected with the ball.*

Onomatopoeia is a type of sensory language, imitating sounds so that the reader can imagine hearing them. It can heighten the reader's involvement in a piece, thus engaging the reader, and it can be taught to children of all ages.

Question

Can you remember the last time you experienced a really long car ride?

Question hooks invoke prior experience, engaging the reader and setting the context for the book. Question hooks are used as beginning techniques in many children's books and are often used in nonfiction text because of their power to access prior knowledge. By first grade, most developing writers can employ question hooks, but questions can grow in depth and complexity as authors mature.

Riddle

What's shaped like a boot, is known as the birthplace of the Renaissance, and contains some of the world's most famous cities?

Riddles are specialized question hooks that awaken any background knowledge the reader may have about a topic. They are great back-door devices for previewing the subtopics that will be addressed in an expository piece and are very effective at engaging readers. Second-grade writers can become proficient with simple riddles. As students grow in abstract reasoning, their riddles can grow in complexity and effectiveness, making this beginning technique very suitable for more advanced young authors.

Setting

A smooth white blanket covered the pasture and feathery snowflakes continued to float silently through the night air.

Writers of both fiction and nonfiction often use a setting description as a beginning technique. They describe time or place in a creative way to draw the reader into the context of the piece. Visual details generate the reader's involvement by stimulating the imagination with pictures.

Clues for inference – Authors paint "word pictures"—allowing readers to put details together to form their own conclusions—rather than making direct statements. Marcia Freeman calls this skill, "Don't hit your reader over the head," drawing attention to the need to allow the reader to make an inference.

The shivering had begun in his toes but had quickly climbed up his back and reached his frozen teeth, causing them to chatter like castanets. He quickly realized the foolishness of setting out with no gloves or hat, as his icy fingers grew stiff and numb and his ears felt like sheets of ice glued to either side of his head.

Rather than telling the reader "he was very cold," the author provides clues and allows the active reader to make an inference. Sometimes called "show, don't tell," this writing-craft skill is best taught to intermediate and secondary writers.

Descriptive attributes – Words used to describe generally refer to some type of attribute of the object being described, like size, shape, color, texture, number, age, composition, or sensory attributes.

*The **century-old** table was **twelve feet long** but very **narrow**, made of **heavy oak** and **wrought iron**.*

Adjectives can describe sensory attributes, such as color, texture, smell, taste, and size, with specific vocabulary. However, caution students to avoid stringing together a series of adjectives. Instead, teach and model the building of a visual image with a focus on descriptive attributes.

Dialogue – Words directly spoken by characters.

***"Remember to use good manners,"** my mother reminded me sternly.*

Dialogue used sparingly and appropriately can help move the plot along while revealing information about the characters. However, some developing writers tend to overuse dialogue. Remind them that readers should not feel as though they are eavesdropping on a conversation; the reader expects the author to *tell the story*.

Dialogue tags – A dialogue tag is a phrase that identifies the speaker.

*"Remember to use good manners," **my mother reminded me sternly.***

Dialogue tags can reveal facets of the character or advance the action of the plot. Overuse of the verb *said* can become monotonous and thereby distracting. However, overindulgence in flowery dialogue tags can also result in distraction. Teach students to add strong verbs and details to their dialogue tags in a purposeful way. When there is no purpose in expanding a tag, a simple *said* or sometimes even tagless dialogue will do.

Embedded definitions – Embedded definitions are the meanings of words or concepts presented within the text. They are most often used in nonfiction but are sometimes used in fiction as well.

Play the piece at an adagio tempo—a moderate "walking" pace.

Readers often learn the meanings of new words and concepts through text. Sometimes, the meaning is implicit. However, sometimes writers place an explicit definition within the text.

Ending techniques – Ending techniques provide students with tools for constructing satisfying conclusions. Students often have difficulty bringing a piece to closure, and learning some common techniques used by authors can help students avoid the "Now you know about..." or "Bye, gotta go now" endings frequently written by children. Some ending techniques common to both fiction and nonfiction follow.

Advice to the reader
The next time you are in the mood for a quick pick-me-up, pick up a crunchy apple and leave the junk food behind.

Writers of fiction and nonfiction often have a final word of advice for the reader. Whether they present a moral of the story, a cautionary word, or a call to action, endings that offer advice add voice to a piece and leave the reader feeling connected to the text and thinking about a way to apply the theme of information presented in their own lives. These endings can be mastered by fluent writers beginning around third grade and grow in complexity and effectiveness as students mature.

Circle back to the hook
Beginning: *Dry leaves swirl around my feet, reminding me that fall has arrived.*

Ending: *Dry leaves swirl around my feet, and I am reminded that fall indeed is here, if only for a while.*

Circling back to the hook means using a technique at the end that is similar to the one used at the beginning. Sometimes the hook is merely echoed and not directly repeated, but still the reader feels that the story has come full circle. These endings can be taught to young authors as soon as they are able to write complete pieces.

Feeling Statement
I love my Grandma.

A feeling statement is a very simple way to bring closure to a personal experience or personal narrative piece. While simple, it is also effective and is an ending technique easily acquired by even the youngest writers.

Question
Young Nicholas knew that he had finally found his treasure—in the pages of a book. Where will you find your treasure?

Question endings invite readers to learn more or to apply what they have learned in the book to new or future experiences. The question might also serve as a very short summary of the main idea. Question endings are generally easy for children to learn to write and are appropriate for young writers.

Remind the reader

Just remember, if you're looking for a state with rich history, fabulous entertainment, and natural beauty, there is no finer destination than Tennessee.

A reminder to the reader is a technique writers use to summarize their main ideas.

This ending technique is most often used in nonfiction writing to review the most important points the author is trying to make. However, it can also be used in fiction texts as a way to leave the reader with a message presented in the story. This technique is appropriate to teach when students begin writing multi-paragraph pieces.

Universal word

***Everybody** needs love.*

Authors sometimes craft conclusions that begin with a universal word, such as *every, all, we, always, everyone.* These words create a generalizing statement that summarizes the author's feelings about the subject or gives the reader a general statement of the theme or central message. These endings are appropriate for writers of all ages.

Hyperbole – Hyperbole refers to a statement using exaggeration for emphasis or effect.

I have about a hundred hours' worth of homework today!

Hyperbole is purposeful exaggeration used to emphasize a point. The reader infers the message without being directly told, understanding that the exaggeration is not meant to be taken literally. Most often used in narratives, hyperbole is most effectively taught to fluent writers who understand figurative language.

Metaphor – A metaphor is a comparison of two unlike things in which the author calls one item or concept by another name so that the reader builds an understanding by forming a visual image. Metaphors are most effectively taught to mature writers who understand figurative language. As the writer matures, metaphors used by the writer can mature as well, creating pieces rich in imagery.

My brother is such a turtle—he'll surely be the last one to finish the race!

By using a metaphor, the author is able to make an implication—like the lack of speed implied in the example above—in an indirect but highly visual manner.

Onomatopoeia – Onomatopoeia refers to words created to imitate sounds.

***Ka-ching**! The cash register rang up another purchase.*

These sound-effects words might be "real words" or can be invented by the author to create a multi-sensory effect. Onomatopoeia is appropriate for even the youngest writers.

Personification – Personification means giving human qualities to non-living or non-human objects.

Angry clouds gathered and began to grumble in protest.

Personification is an effective descriptive technique, helping the reader visualize and connect with text. Because personification is a type of figurative language, both creating and interpreting it require higher-order thinking skills. Therefore, this skill is best taught to fluent readers and writers in late elementary years and beyond.

Repetition – Repetition occurs when authors repeat words, phrases, or sentences.

For twelve hours, the only thing we could count on was rain, rain, and more rain.

Repetition is frequently used in poetry, often used in narrative writing, and sometimes used in expository writing. It can establish rhythm in a piece of writing and add a sense comfortable predictability for the reader. Repetition can be effectively taught to all levels of writers.

Rhyme – Rhyme is the repetition of the middle and ending sounds of words.

There he sat—lonely Joe with nowhere to go.

Rhyme is most often associated with poetry and books for young readers. It creates a pattern with sounds and a sense of anticipation and predictability. For emergent writers, teaching rhyme can yield reciprocal reading benefits, as rhyme is associated with phonemic awareness and word families. Fluent writers can analyze rhyme patterns in poetry and learn to apply rhyme schemes as a vehicle for creating mood and supporting meaning.

Sentence variation – Writers intentionally vary the form and length of sentences within a piece.

At first the deer stood frozen like a statue between trees. But then it flinched. Its head rose. Was it suddenly aware of my presence?

Young writers can vary the length of their sentences by adding phrases and clauses to expand a sentence. They learn to vary sentence types, sprinkling questions and exclamations into their writing. As they mature, students learn to construct compound and complex sentences. Sentence variation keeps readers engaged in a piece of writing.

Simile – A simile is a comparison of unlike entities using the words *like* or *as*.

The rain bounced on the concrete like ping pong balls on a tile floor.

A simile is a literary device used to create imagery through comparison. Similes help the reader create visual images. Similes can be taught to mature writers who understand figurative language (usually around second grade).

Specificity – Specificity refers to the use of specific common and proper nouns.

He ate a bowl of Wheaties® soaked in skim milk.

Specificity means writing *Walmart* instead of *store* and *roses* instead of *flowers*. By using specificity, writers help readers visualize and connect to text. This skill is most effectively taught beginning in second or third grade, when students learn to distinguish common and proper nouns, but students of all ages can benefit from exposure to specificity.

Strong verbs – Strong verbs are action verbs that are specific and easily visualized by the reader.

The mockingbird ***swooped*** *and* ***screeched, chasing*** *the hawk away from her nest.*

Strong verbs are important to every genre because they help readers create visual images. They are an essential element of lively, engaging text. Strong verbs can be effectively taught to every level of writer. However, if the term *verb* has not been introduced, teachers can refer to strong verbs as *action words* or *words that tell what's happening.*

Supporting details – Supporting details form the substance of expository writing; they provide the evidence necessary to convince the reader that the *author* is truly an *author*ity and that the information and arguments presented are valid. Most supporting details will fall into these categories:

- Facts – *School attendance is mandatory in the United States.*
- Self-evident truths – *Well-organized people don't waste a lot of time searching for lost items.*
- Anecdotes (narrative vignettes) – *Last year, I had a serious bicycle accident. My head struck the ground with such force that I required emergency medical care for a concussion. Fortunately, my helmet saved me from more serious injury.*
- Comparisons or analogies – *A moth emerges from a fuzzy cocoon; a butterfly, however, emerges from a hard, slick skin called a chrysalis.*
- Authoritative quotes or testimonials – *My tennis coach repeatedly reminds me: "Racket back and down!"*
- Numbers/statistics – *Experts estimate that sixty-five percent of the solid waste in existing landfills is made of paper that could have been recycled.*
- Descriptive details – *Bumblebees are large, hairy insects with a loud, humming buzz and an awkward flight style. Most of them can be easily identified by the familiar black and yellow stripes.*
- Definitions – *Ants have strong mandibles, or jaws.*
- Graphics (diagrams, maps, charts, bulleted lists, etc.)

Marcia S. Freeman colorfully illustrates the need for supporting details by invoking the image of school-age cynics on the playground: *Oh, yeah? Prove it!* When making a statement—whether of personal talent or public service—she suggests teaching students to use a variety of supporting details to "prove it!"

Transitional devices - Transitional devices signal changes. In informational writing, transitions often occur when a new supporting idea is presented or when items need to be ordered (*First of all, Another reason, Equally important is, For example, On the other hand, Similarly,* etc.). In narratives, transitions often signal changes in place and time. The following types of transitions are commonly taught beginning in the early elementary years. As students mature, their transitions become more precise and detailed.

Changes in place
When she reached the parking lot, she realized her mistake.

Place transitions help the reader follow the movements of a character or changes in the setting. They include words and phrases such as *at school, across the ocean, inside the cave,* and the like.

Changes in time
At 3:00, the bell rang and students poured from the classrooms.

Time transitions are cues that signal a change in time. They include words and phrases such as *the next day, after breakfast, when darkness came,* and the like. They are most often found in narratives, where they give order to the reader by showing the passage of time, and in procedural writing.

Voice – Voice is the unique style of an author's language.

You might hear some say this town is dull. You won't hear me say that, no siree.

Voice manifests itself in the word choice, tone, style, imagery, and rhythm of language created by an author. While this mature trait is a little nebulous and difficult to explicitly teach, students should be continually exposed to various authors' voices, and can be taught some specific techniques that will help them develop their own voices as writers.

Immersing Students in Craft

As your students are exposed to high-quality literature—through their independent reading, your read-alouds, and literature models used during writing instruction—they will realize that they are surrounded by craft. Naming that craft and teaching students *what writers know* will awaken their critical-thinking skills, and students will begin to identify craft elements by name.

A good resource for your professional library is the second edition of *Models for Teaching Writing-craft Target Skills* (Maupin House, 2010), a book co-authored by Marcia S. Freeman and myself. This book includes multiple matrices for easily locating writing-craft skills in well-known children's books and poetry, including nonfiction and Spanish-language literature models.

Keep running lists of craft examples in your classroom. Put them on chart paper and make lists accessible to students so they can add examples of craft from their own reading. These lists should be fluid and dynamic. Once you have introduced a skill, build and maintain the concept by allowing students to take ownership of lists and feel intangibly rewarded for recognizing craft in their reading.

As students write, you may want to collect examples of craft from their writing as well and list them on chart paper, class reward charts, teacher-made resources, or your website. The excitement will grow and take on its own momentum as your students see craft exploding from the literature that surrounds them.

Use the interactive glossary found in the **Appendix** to reinforce craft skills with your students. As you are teaching the skills, students can write the definitions and either create their own examples of the craft skills or quote the craft from literature models.

Genre Instruction

Modern writing curricula are very genre centered. Students practice writing and are assessed within various modes of writing. Many writing-craft skills are applicable to every genre. For instance, strong verbs, descriptive language, specificity, and sentence variation will equally enhance the quality of a personal narrative or an informational piece.

Other writing-craft skills are generally confined to a specific genre. For instance, time and place transitions are most often found in narratives. Transitions that add information or set up comparisons are generally used in expository writing.

As you plan for instruction, select writing-craft skills that can work together within a genre. Teach the skills in isolation, using literature models, teacher models, and interactive practice. Allow your students to practice the skills in small groups, pairs, and individually so that they will gain proficiency with each skill before expecting them to apply multiple skills in a genre piece.

After teaching a group of individual writing-craft skills, assign a genre piece in which students will apply the entire group of skills. Your students will feel a sense of command over the craft, and you will have a set of criteria to help you assess the finished piece with inherent objectivity.

The genre groups most often taught and/or assessed in schools are **descriptive writing**, **narrative writing**, **expository writing**, **opinion and persuasive writing,** and **poetry**. Within each genre, several subgroups can be identified. As you consider your long-range plans for an academic year, identify the genres and subgroups of genres that you will teach.

After identifying the genres and subgroups, look at the writing-craft skills listed and defined above. Sort the skills among genre groups to set up your scope and sequence. Be sure to revisit skills after they are taught. For instance, you may include strong verbs in your descriptive writing unit, but don't hesitate to include them again in narrative writing and poetry. Writing-craft skills should continually cycle back into your instructional framework.

Descriptive Writing

Descriptive writing is a good place to start. The focus of descriptive writing is creating images that readers can visualize. Of course, this is central to well-crafted writing in any genre. If you begin your year with a descriptive writing unit, you will be able to cover many skills that will be revisited in other genres.

While descriptive skills can be applied in many genres, descriptive writing is distinct. It is built on observation, not plot or information. The subject of a descriptive piece can range from a person or setting to an emotion or event.

Descriptive writing is generally rich with sensory language and attention to detail. For many students, adjectives are synonymous with description. By focusing an instructional unit on descriptive writing, you can dispel this myth.

While a descriptive piece may be teeming with adjectives, it will probably also include figurative language, such as similes, metaphors, hyperboles, and personification. Strong verbs will aid the reader's visualization and sentence variation will keep the reader engaged.

Planning. When planning a descriptive unit, it is usually helpful to begin assembling picture prompts. Cut up old calendars and greeting cards. Tear interesting pictures out of magazines. Take photographs of areas of beauty and interest on your school campus.

Individual photographs of students, self-portraits, and art projects are also meaningful catalysts for descriptive writing. As always, try to keep the topics relevant and motivating to your students.

Descriptive pieces are often brief, like a character sketch or a free-verse nature poem. They can be of moderate length, like a one-page description of a famous painting or a descriptive character analysis written as a literature response.

When assigning a brief descriptive piece as practice, model the process for writing by working collectively to construct a piece with your students. The following free-verse descriptive poem was written as a collective model for the setting description activity:

Beneath the sheltering canopy of trees
Smooth, glossy stones shimmer
With fragments of golden sunlight.
Glassy water rolls slowly, softly,
Like a lullaby.
Emerald leaves sparkle overhead
And long, soft grasses cushion
The deep muddy banks
Of the creek at Stone Mountain.

This setting description activity, provided for you in the **Appendix** of this book, builds descriptive skills while letting students review and apply knowledge of parts of speech. Students can work with you to construct a collective model to a picture prompt. Following this interactive exercise, students are ready to work independently to create their own free-verse poems to a picture you have provided or they have selected. Students can even write about settings they have drawn:

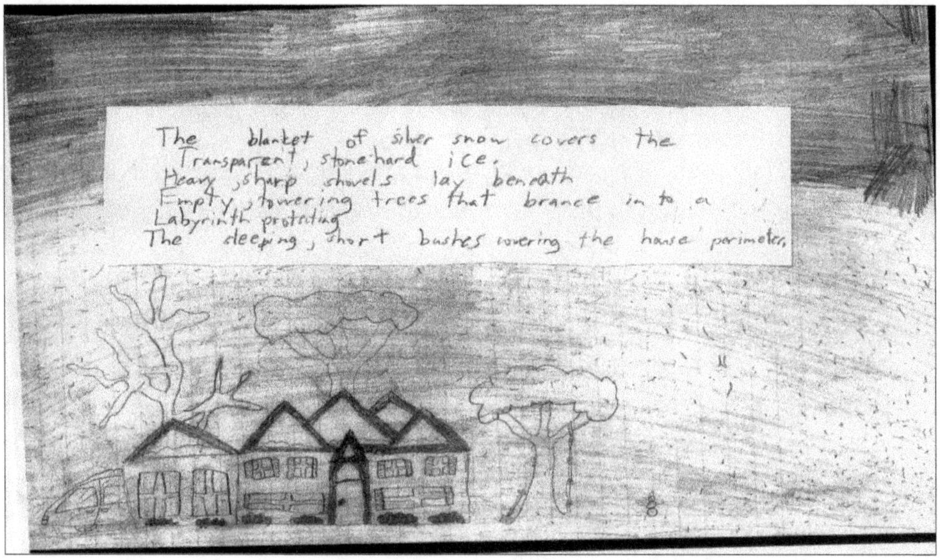

KEVIN, FIFTH GRADE

Similarly, descriptions of artwork, characters, school events, and local points of interest can become the subject of this type of descriptive piece. Teach students that descriptive pieces are "word portraits." They paint pictures in the mind of the reader. For practice in describing characters, work collectively to describe the subject of a famous portrait (see the **Appendix** for a character description activity), and then give students the task of self-description.

Capitalize on the potential for integrating writing with content areas by having students complete this exercise with pictures related to your science or social studies curriculum. Descriptive writing can be built from empirical observation in science, or from data collected while researching a geographical location or a famous figure in history.

After writing brief pieces, students are comfortable launching into lengthier descriptive pieces. Teach them to be keen observers and to take notes on their observations. These notes become the details around which the descriptive piece will be written. Students can sort and classify the observed details to form paragraphs.

Once they have surveyed the information that will be included in body paragraphs, students can form a thesis statement on which to build the introduction and conclusion. In this way, students gain proficiency with descriptive writing a little at a time. By the time they are writing a lengthy descriptive piece, their confidence will be strong and the genre will not seem vague or intimidating.

Narrative Writing

Narratives are stories containing characters, settings, and a chronological sequence of events. Time passes and the ending drives the story. Like a set of travel directions, the plot travels from event to event in a constant forward movement toward the climactic event and subsequent denouement—the gentle, unraveling fall to a conclusion.

Authors almost always write narratives in past tense, recounting events after they have already occurred. Point this out to students and make them conscious of consistent tense. They will have greater control over their writing if we teach them to keep their narratives in the past tense.

There are two types of narratives: fictional and personal. Fictional narratives are created stories that usually revolve around a central conflict. The point of view is generally either first person—told from the perspective of a main character—or third person—told by a narrator.

Personal narratives are written in first-person point of view. The main character is reflective, moving the reader through a series of events to ultimately reveal what he or she learned, achieved, or realized.

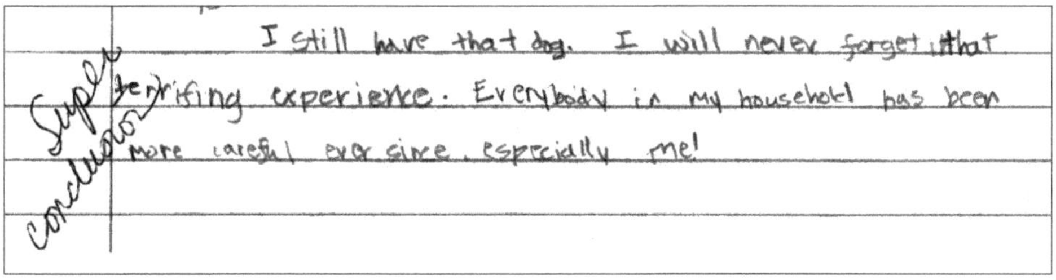

NARRATIVE ENDING: REFLECTIVE - BRITTANY, FIFTH GRADE

Planning. For either type of narrative, the planning is similar. The bulk of the story occurs in the middle, sandwiched between a brief introduction and a neat, satisfying, and similarly brief conclusion. The middle portion of the story is planned by creating a sequential list of events.

This sequence of events should flow logically from one event to the next. The plot should not be rushed. Ideally, events should unfold with visual description, dramatic tension, and incremental revelations of characters and plot. Of course, the maturity of the writers will dictate the intricacy of the plot.

Graphic organizers should be linear and emphasize the importance of keep the beginning and ending brief. For personal narratives, a very simple structure is appropriate. Using first-person point of view, the author can introduce the setting and focal event or emotion in the beginning.

The sequence of events can be listed as bulleted fragments in the middle of the plan. I usually encourage students to leave space between events so they can go back and fill in connecting events as needed.

The ending of a personal narrative generally reveals a personal change, a sense of accomplishment, a lesson learned, or a reflective emotion felt by the story's persona. Because the ending drives the narrative, it is important for students to determine the type of ending they will use during the planning stage.

You may find it effective to have students plan the beginning and ending of a personal narrative prior to listing the sequence of events in the middle. Particularly when students have difficulty with organization, this strategy helps them identify a destination and the planning becomes a very convergent process.

The following is an example of a very simple graphic organizer that can be made by having students fold the top and bottom quarters of a paper to create three sections. If you prefer using a template, one is included in the **Appendix**. As you can see, the linear nature of the planning device makes it ideal for narratives, and the sections help the writer focus on a brief beginning and end.

B:
M:
E:

This graphic organizer can also be used with fictional narratives. However, you may want to create a more plot-controlled fictional narrative planner, especially with younger writers. A folded, eight-section graphic organizer can help students structure a tight, focused fictional narrative.

The eight boxes give students spaces for planning the title, main character(s), setting(s), problem/central conflict, attempts to solve the problem/resolve the conflict, and a conclusion. When discussing these story elements, I usually ask students to help me retell a widely known folktale and then model the construction of a graphic organizer for that story:

Title:	**Character(s):**	**Setting(s):**	**Problem:**
The Three Little Pigs	*First Pig* *Second Pig* *Third Pig* *Big Bad Wolf*	*The Woods –* *Straw house* *Stick house* *Brick house*	*Pigs want to live in peace, but wolf wants to eat them.*
Event #1:	**Event #2:**	**Event #3:**	**Conclusion:**
Wolf goes to straw house. Pig won't let him in. Wolf blows house down. Pig runs to brother's house.	*Wolf goes to stick house. Pigs won't let him in. Wolf blows house down. Pigs run to brother's house.*	*Wolf goes to brick house. Pigs won't let him in. Wolf can't blow house down. Goes down chimney. Boiling water.*	*Pigs lived happily and peacefully in brick house never bothered by big bad wolf again.*

Storyboards can also be effective ways to organize narratives, especially for younger writers. Even with intermediate-age writers, sketching can be a very useful planning tool and can lead to easily visualized writing. Storyboards can be made by folding a paper into quarters and sketching the main events in each box.

1	**2**
3	**4**

When using storyboards, I always encourage students to plan the first and last blocks before planning the two middle events. Once again, it is important for students to begin with the end in mind.

Beyond planning, there are many important skills to introduce, model, and practice when teaching narratives. Writers choose from a variety of beginning techniques to hook the reader (e.g., *onomatopoeia, question, setting, dialogue, exclamation, mystery/suspense,* etc.).

The following beginning to a narrative piece, written by a fifth-grade student, provides an example of setting used as a beginning technique. The young author begins from a broad perspective and narrows in on the specific setting for her story.

112 Broken Moon Lane

If you happened to be flying very low over the huge state of Minnesota, you would see an ordinary town called Blackson. If you flew a little lower, you would find an ordinary street called Broken Moon Lane. And you would catch a glimpse of Number 112, where you might see a not-so-ordinary family, Abby, Nick, and Jasmine Seir.

BEGINNING TECHNIQUE: SETTING - ERIN, FIFTH GRADE

Beginning a story with a dialogue lead can give the reader a sense of immediacy. The action has already begun and the reader is being thrust into the situation:

"Why are guys always so stupid?" yelled Jessi fiercely. "That's it, Drew McCoy, I'm never talking to you again!" She started towards the McCoy's basement door as her dark blond ponytail swayed behind her as if it were following her out the door.

BEGINNING TECHNIQUE: DIALOGUE - DARBI, FIFTH GRADE

The style of a narrative, along with the author's chosen voice, can be introduced in a clever lead that shifts the reader's mind into genre and mood, like this lead to a student's tall tale:

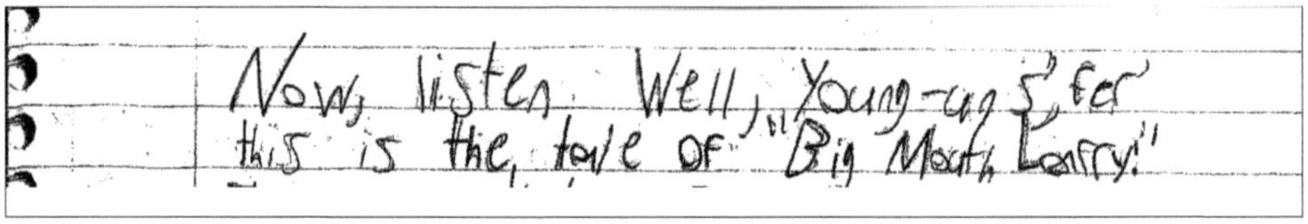
Now, listen. Well, Young-uns, for this is the tale of "Big Mouth Larry!"

BEGINNING TECHNIQUE: ADDRESSING THE READER - TOMMY, FIFTH GRADE

After a compelling lead, the author has led the reader into the narrative and can begin to build the plot. Mini-lessons and literature models can help young writers construct concepts like rising action, climactic events, and falling action as they devote the bulk of their workshop time to composition.

Paragraphing in narratives occurs when there are changes in *place, action, time,* or *speaker*. (Marcia Freeman suggests the use of the acronym *PATS* to guide the paragraphing of narratives.) Changes in speaker are obvious, but changes in place and time are marked by transitional devices. Because time passes and characters may move between settings, narratives usually rely heavily on transitions that indicate changes in *time* and *place.*

Time transitions might be general (*Later; Another time*; *On a separate occasion*) or specific (*At 4:00; As the sunk sank low in the western sky; When the dismissal bell rang*). Place transitions can move the character within a setting (*As I sat down at my desk; I walked to the window; She moved closer to the beehive*) or from one setting to another (*When I got to school; By the time she reached the bus stop; At the mall*).

Narrative endings can take many forms (e.g., lesson learned, goal achieved, reflective thoughts, circle back to the hook, feelings statement, etc.) but must give the reader a sense that loose ends are tied up and the story has settled to a satisfying conclusion.

> *I found out that it doesn't matter what people think of you. Just be happy with yourself. I learned that I should just be happy taking the slow road.*

NARRATIVE ENDING: LESSON LEARNED - JAKE, FOURTH GRADE

> *Everyone shouted, "Dribble! You're back! We missed you!" We played for hours. It was great to be back home.*

NARRATIVE ENDING: FEELINGS STATEMENT - TANNER, FOURTH GRADE

In fictional narratives, the ending often assures the reader that the threat is gone:

> BigMouth Larry was just like the tornader he made: a lone wolf, always on the move, and makin' a heck' load of noise! But, what's that? WHAT happened to that tornado he talked up? Well, it was SO big, and SO strong, it went ALL the way to Kansas, where it picked up a small farm-girl, and a tiny yappin' dog, and brought them all the way to a magical land, where witches are real, scarecrows can talk, and lions are cowardly. But that tale, my friends, is a 'nother story...

FICTIONAL NARRATIVE ENDING - TOMMY, FIFTH GRADE

Before you embark on a narrative unit of instruction, identify the skills you will teach, the mentor texts from which you will model those skills, and the planning devices you will direct your students to use. Once you have gathered these tools, you will be equipped to help your students develop meaningful, well-constructed narratives.

Expository Writing

Expository writing has a distinct purpose. These pieces are written to inform, explain, compare, or persuade. It is the type of writing students will most likely be required to create or comprehend throughout their lives.

Unlike narrative writing, expository writing is not organized chronologically (with the exception of procedural writing). Expository writing is characterized by thesis statements and groups of related details. Details are arranged in groups that support the author's main ideas. Tense and point of view vary.

Planning. Different forms of expository writing may use different types of pre-writing, planning, transitions, and paragraphing strategies. For example, comparison writing relies heavily on critical-thinking skills. Graphic organizers include the Venn diagram and the *CraftPlus* Comparison Organizer (see **Appendix**). Students need to identify attributes of each object of comparison and sort the ways the objects are similar and different according to each of the identified attributes.

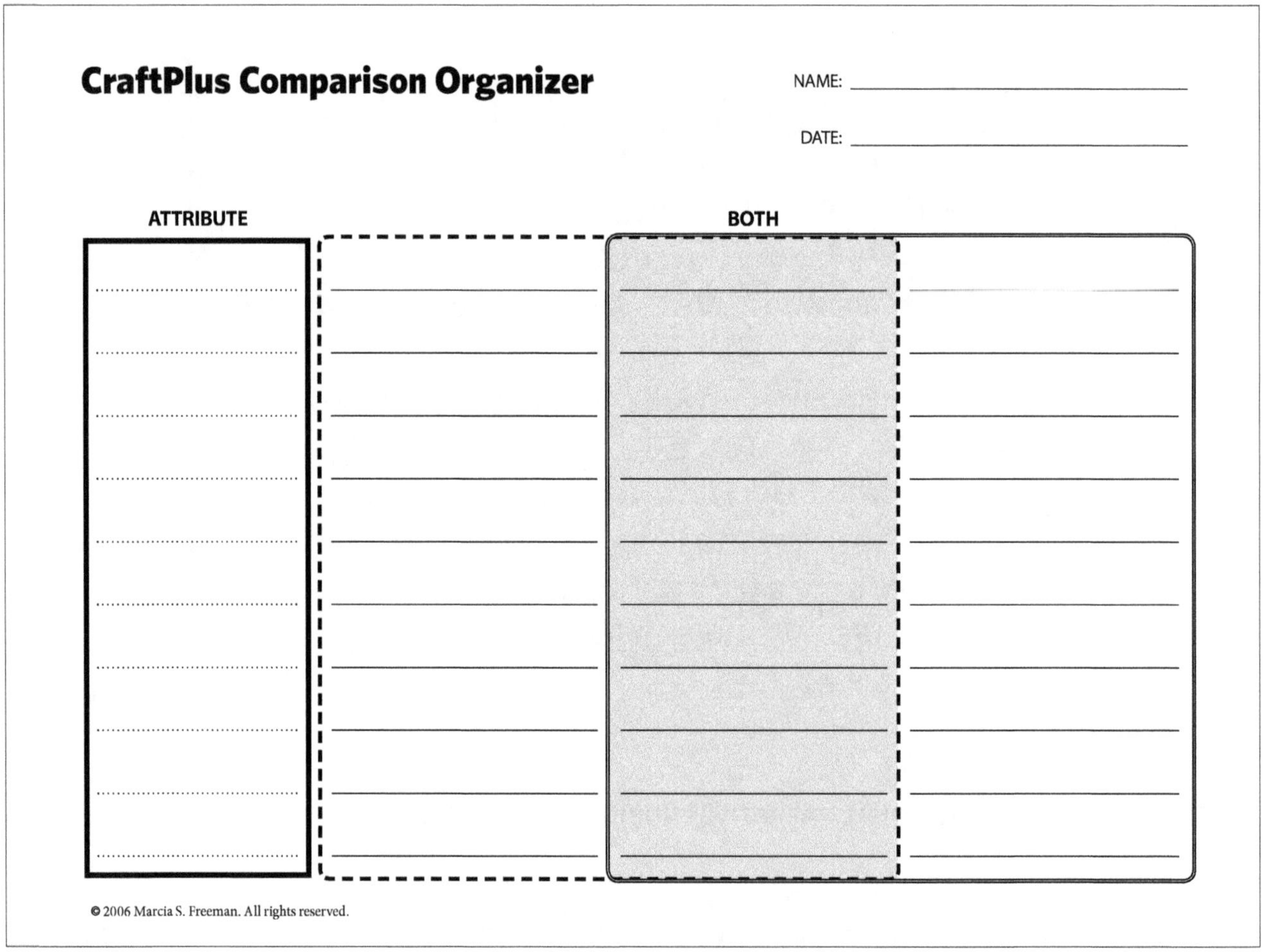

CRAFTPLUS COMPARISON ORGANIZER

Most expository writing is best planned by listing details and sorting them into related groups. Concept webs and flow charts are often used to help students form sets of details:

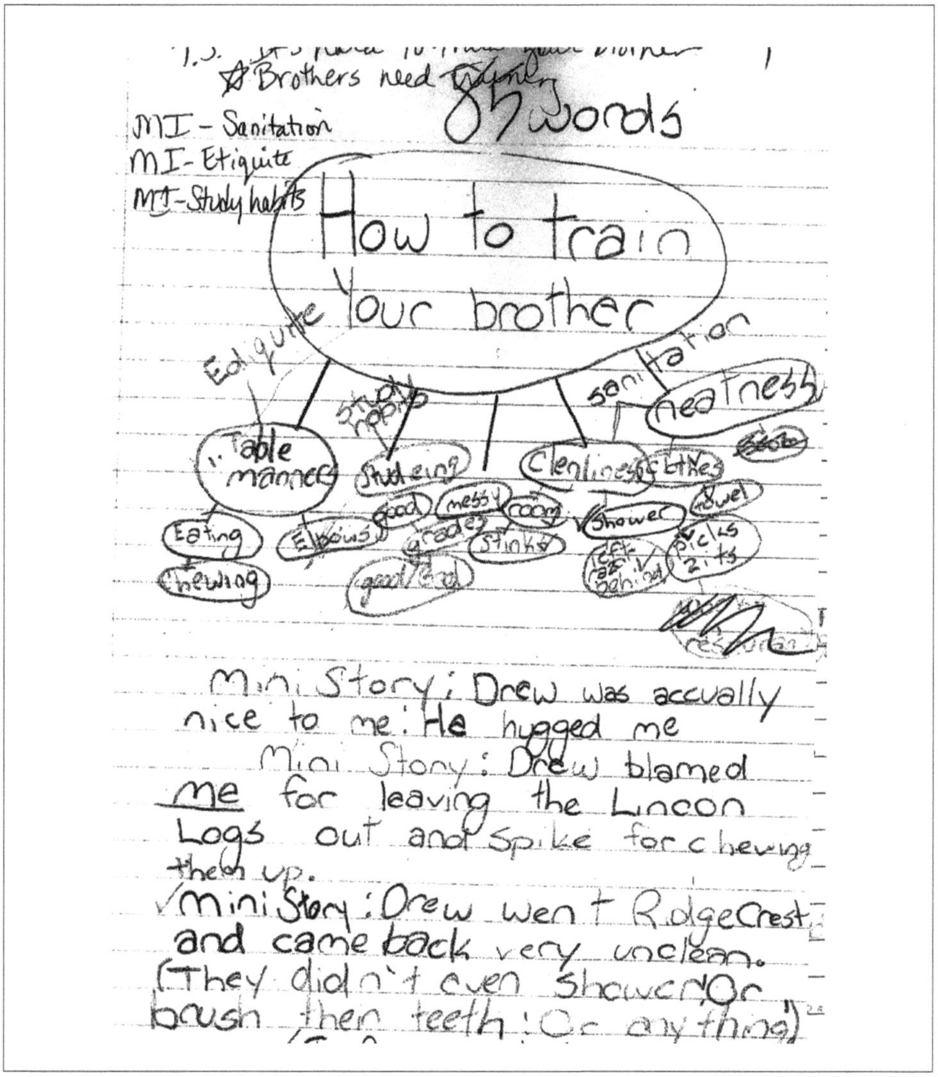

CONCEPT WEB AND PLAN FOR SUPPORTING DETAILS – LILY, FOURTH GRADE

Informational expository pre-writing should focus on details. Whether generated through brainstorming, conversation, or research, the details must be collected and pooled together before planning can begin. Once details are spread out before the author, the planning can start.

Details must be categorized and grouped. The main ideas for each group provide the topic of each body paragraph within the informational expository piece. Pieces written to *explain why* are organized in this same manner. Persuasive writing is organized similarly, but there are so many intricacies to this mode of writing that we will address it separately.

Expository pieces should be organized with an *introduction*, a *body*, and a *conclusion*. Like narrative pieces, the beginning and end should be brief; unlike narratives, expository introductions and conclusions should introduce and reinforce the thesis.

Prior to introducing the thesis, writers of expository pieces choose from a variety of beginning techniques to hook the reader (e.g., *onomatopoeia, question, scenario, startling fact, exclamation, global-to-specific statement*). A compelling beginning hooks the reader, and the thesis follows.

> *What?! You don't think that ants are amazing?! With huge numbers per colony they're practically just like us! To list two similarities, they live in houses and they can wage war. Listen as I teach you about the wonders of ants.*

"AMAZING ANTS" - KEVIN, FIFTH GRADE

Other than the introduction and conclusion, paragraphing in expository writing occurs when there is a *change in the main idea for a group of related details*. Expository transitions generally fall into these categories: additive (*another thought, furthermore, in addition*), incidence (*usually, frequently, occasionally*), emphasis (*once again, to repeat, to reiterate*), and cause and effect (*as a result, because, consequently*).

Expository ending techniques usually *remind the reader of the main point, tell where to find more information*, or *give advice*.

> *There are many unique Ancient Greek pots, but each and every one has a special purpose. For more information, you can go to these websites: www.greece.mrdonn.org and www.ancientgreece.co.uk.*

EXPOSITORY ENDING: WHERE TO FIND MORE INFORMATION - HILLARY, THIRD GRADE

> *Being a teacher is about shaping the future of your students, giving them a hand in preparing themselves for the life ahead of them, and creating an enjoyable learning environment for each and every child, and this is exactly what I am striving to achieve.*

EXPOSITORY ENDING: REMIND THE READER OF MAIN POINTS - DYLAN, COLLEGE STUDENT

> *Take it from me, if you want to save yourself a lot of trouble, just do your chores.*

EXPOSITORY ENDING: ADVICE TO THE READER - FOURTH GRADE

Newspapers and age-appropriate magazines are potent literature models for expository writing-craft skills. In addition to modeling these skills while teaching, allow children to locate expository beginning and ending techniques, transitions, and other writing-craft skills used in these resources. As you model writing craft from these resources, be sure to pay attention to the structure of each piece—how the information is presented and the way main ideas and groups of details form body paragraphs.

Some students come to expository writing with the predetermined idea that there *must* be three body paragraphs. However, there is no set number of paragraphs required in an expository piece, and we should clarify for students that while three body paragraphs are very common, two well-supported body paragraphs or four well-planned body paragraphs can be equally good or even better.

The only absolute is that *details* should guide the organization of a well-written expository piece. If students begin by corralling all of the bits and pieces of information they have on the topic and then organize those details into groups, they are ready to write an expository piece.

Opinion and Persuasive Writing

Persuasive writing is a very specific form of expository, written with the express purpose of convincing the reader to share the author's perspective. Persuasive and opinion writing are often taught together, but the two are not synonymous. Opinion pieces present the writer's viewpoint, but persuasive pieces seek to alter the reader's opinion. Because of this relationship, opinion skills should precede instruction in persuasive writing.

The first step is to make sure students have a clear understanding of fact vs. opinion. From that point, students can explore and narrow topics, perform research and collect data, and plan for writing. As with other expository forms of writing, students should begin with the supporting details and organize them into related groups, each with its own thesis statement.

Younger students enjoy writing opinion papers about *favorites*—favorite season, favorite activity, favorite subject, etc. The focus is on their own likes and dislikes. Developing supporting details in these pieces involves creating a personal list of *reasons why*. In the process, students learn to articulate a rationale for their personal preferences, which is a critical-thinking skill.

With younger writers, instruction in supporting details should focus on types of evidence, such as *facts, personal vignettes, authoritative quotes,* and *concrete examples.* More mature writers should learn about *valid vs. unsubstantiated evidence, organization of arguments,* and *comparison skills.*

In persuasive, pieces, supporting details must present a convincing argument to the reader—bits of evidence strong enough to sway the reader's opinion. Persuasive writing can be effective using first-, second-, or third-person perspective but is often written in second person to directly address the reader.

Exercise can make you stronger. You can have bulging muscles like a super-hero. With those muscles, you'll easily be able to lift 50-pound weights or everyday items as well. Working out can make you excel at sports, too. For example, baseball requires arm muscles for batting, a strong throwing arm, powerful legs for running, and overall endurance needed by all athletes. So, exercise and impress your friends!

SECOND-PERSON POINT OF VIEW - WRITTEN COLLECTIVELY BY A FIFTH-GRADE CLASS AND TEACHER

Planning. Both opinion and persuasive pieces should be organized with an *introduction*, a *body,* and a *closing*. Writers choose from a variety of beginning techniques to create an introduction that hooks the reader (e.g., *question, scenario, startling fact, description, anecdote, global-to-specific statement*). The body paragraphs should present arguments and supporting details, and the closing should leave the reader with something to think about. Ending techniques often *summarize*, *make a prediction*, *make a recommendation*, or *circle back to the hook.*

Other than the introduction and closing, paragraphing in opinion and persuasive writing occurs when there is a *change in the main idea for a group of related details*. Transitions generally fall into these categories: additive (*another thought, furthermore, in addition*), incidence (*usually, frequently, occasionally*), comparison (*similarly, conversely, on the other hand*), emphasis (*once again, to repeat, to reiterate*), and cause and effect (*as a result, because, consequently*).

Graphic organizers of many varieties can help students plan their persuasive pieces. Concept webs and flow charts can help them sort details into related groups for constructing thesis statements and well-supported arguments. Since persuasive writers should address the opposition, it is often helpful for students to use T-charts (like the one here), listing pros and cons or comparing their position of the opposition.

Whether the piece is meant to express the author's opinion or persuade the reader, supporting details are foundational. After that, descriptive skills will help the reader visualize and connect to the text, and organizational skills will provide clarity. Prior to teaching opinion or persuasive writing, select the writing-craft skills you want students to employ. Model and practice those skills, and then allow students to apply them.

Procedural Writing

Procedural writing, often called "how-to" writing, provides steps in a process. It is the only form of expository writing organized chronologically (rather than as groups of related details) because the reader must follow an organized sequence of steps to achieve the desired result.

Procedural pieces contain a few integral parts: an objective, sequential steps, and transitions that put those steps in order. Descriptive writing skills are applied in a way that makes the task easier to achieve because the reader can visualize the process.

Most of your students' writing will be done from either the first-person or third-person perspective. It is rare for students to write pieces written from the second-person point of view, but this rare perspective is used in most procedural pieces.

When assigning a procedural piece, the process and objective should be within the realm of your students' experience. Making sandwiches, playing board games, and finding a location in your school are common themes of procedural pieces.

Planning. While the planning is always linear, the end result of a procedural writing piece can be organized in many different formats. Your students can write multi-paragraph pieces, organizing the steps as paragraphs and providing ample description and specificity. They may also be organized as detailed lists, sequencing steps with enumeration.

Many procedural themes lend themselves to integration with art. Students can draw maps to accompany a piece that gives directions to a location, or they can design their own games, creating game boards, pawns, and games cards.

Students usually enjoy creating comic strips, and procedural writing is an ideal genre for "boxing" in linear fashion. Simply fold a piece of paper to make four boxes, or cut a long strip of craft paper and fold it to make a row of squares.

The following comic strips each contain four boxes identifying steps in a process; one piece explains the procedure for playing the game Four Square, and the other tells how to make an electromagnet. In each, illustrations provide the details and prompt the reader's visualization. Brief, direct statements guide the reader through the steps of the process. Comic strips like these can be the end product for a procedural assignment or can serve as a storyboard for planning a procedural piece..

"HOW TO PLAY FOUR-SQUARE" – DARBI, FIFTH GRADE

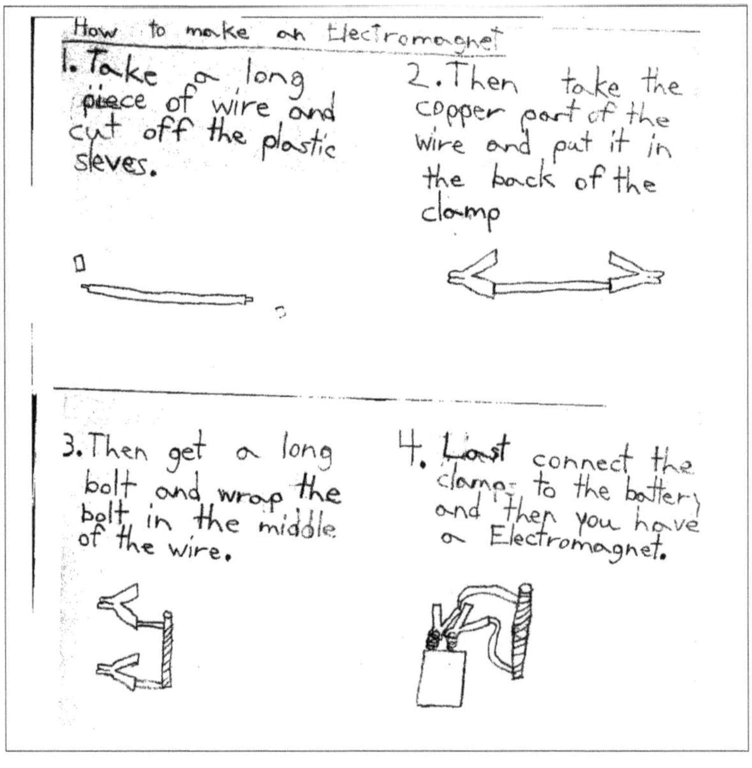

"HOW TO MAKE AN ELECTROMAGNET" – MICHAEL, FIFTH GRADE

Poetry

Poetry provides an opportunity for reluctant writers to feel a sense of freedom from the rules of prose and gives all students a chance to feel a sense of accomplishment without the labor and time investment of expository or narrative compositions. Poetry can be an enriching personal experience for students and may even serve as a portal to applying descriptive skills in prose.

Poetry is often taught as a isolated genre but is beneficial to teach throughout the year as well. For teachers, a poetry unit can provide a great opportunity to review the writing craft taught during the school year in a fresh, new way. Individual writing-craft skills can be reinforced and even assessed through poetry.

Consider the power of using poetry to teach or reinforce figurative language, like similes, metaphors, and personification. Poetry models are easy to find—this genre is teeming with figurative language. You will find that young children begin to imitate the imagery of poetry before they have learned the names of literary devices. This intuitive imagery lays a foundation for acquisition of and facility with craft skills when they are formally introduced. Model craft skills through poems and then have students apply the skills in original free-verse pieces.

Observe the way the application of metaphor matures in the following progression of student samples:

"STARS": FREE-VERSE POEM USING COMPARISONS - JOSEPH, KINDERGARTEN

"The Solar System"

The sun is a great big juggler;
all of the planets go
around and around.
The earth, the moons,
Saturn, Venus and so much more --
you might be able to see it!
It's a lovely sight!

"THE SOLAR SYSTEM": METAPHOR POEM - DEAN, SECOND GRADE

"THE SOUL": METAPHOR POEM - RUBY, FOURTH GRADE

"Earthworms!!"

Little pink explorers,
You make tunnels in the ground,
Going past the bugs and rocks,
Heading down, down, down...
You do not EAT the dirt,
But really what's inside it,
MICROSCOPIC PARASITES,
That's your daily diet.
You soften up the dirt for us
So we can make our gardens,
I really HATE IT when you go,
For then the soil hardens.
Unfortunately, not everyone loves you,
I've heard some call you vile.
But when I see you...
I CANNOT HELP BUT SMILE!

METAPHOR POEM - TOMMY, FIFTH GRADE

Formats of poetry are very popular. While they give students patterns that help make the writing process more concrete, poetry formats do not always lend themselves to the development of writing craft. Craft often becomes secondary to the constraints of the format. This doesn't mean we shouldn't use them; but when using formats, be clear in forming your instructional objectives.

For example, diamantes are terrific vehicles for reviewing parts of speech. You can teach and practice rhyme, rhythm, and syllables with couplets or quatrains. Haikus apply syllable knowledge and force students to shrink writing to the bare necessities because there is no room for extra words. Limericks can be challenging and fun as well.

Tiffany Lee:

There once was a night with no moon
We hoped it would come really soon
We lay in the dark
Then hear a late lark
Then suddenly it was noon

LIMERICK - TIFFANY, FIFTH GRADE

Infuse poetry into your writing curriculum throughout the year. While rhythm and rhyme can be fun, expose students to free-verse, unrhymed poetry as well. The focus of writing should remain, as much as possible, on the descriptive and expressive nature of language.

Letter Writing

Letter writing is not actually a genre but a format for writing. The style and purpose of a letter might lead to narrative, expository, or descriptive writing. While the purpose for writing may vary, the friendly letter format is usually taught in the elementary school years.

Dear Mom and Dad,

Don't you think it would be a marvelous idea to let me make dinner? Before you say no, listen to this. You will say yes!

First, I think you should proudly know that I would make it delicious, but healthy. If I made this low-calorie meal, I would make salad. You will want it again. I'll even wash the dishes after we are all finished eating.

Now you are probably thinking that I will get burnt on the stove or the oven. Don't worry, I won't even use those. I will make a perfectly safe and nutritious meal. I promise to wash my hands first.

The one thing that you cannot say no to is that there will gladly be no mess. (At least not for you to clean up.) Our plates will be perfectly clean by the time we are finished eating.

I hope I get to make dinner some time. If I make dinner once, I'll be making it again, and again, and again.

Love,
Hillary

FRIENDLY LETTER: PERSUASIVE - HILLARY, THIRD GRADE

Aside from friendly letters, teach students to write business letters, invitations, and thank-you notes as well. Students can select companies to which they would like to send business letters, offering a suggestion for a new product, providing marketing advice, or asking questions.

Invitations and thank-you notes can become a part of classroom events. Students can formally invite their parents to programs or send invitations to "little buddies" in a lower grade, inviting them to a read-athon or holiday celebration. Thank-you notes can routinely follow field trip providers and guest speakers; notes of gratitude are often greatly appreciated by food service workers, custodial staff, and your school's administration.

The primary purpose of writing is communication. There is no more authentic form of written communication than the letter. Use this wonderfully purposeful format to nurture the concept of writing for your students.

Long-range Planning

Before the start of your school year, determine the genres and formats appropriate for your grade level. Then look at a calendar and decide when you will teach each individual genre. If there are standardized writing assessments required by your school or district, you will want to be sure to equip students with the skills necessary to meet the test criteria.

For example, if your students will be required to respond to an expository prompt for an assessment in January, you will want to be sure to teach descriptive writing skills and expository writing skills thoroughly sometime during the first semester, allow time to review essential expository skills, and introduce your students to the testing format prior to the assessment.

Your next consideration should be events and units of study. Aim to integrate writing into your content-area instruction so that learning will be meaningful and connected. You may want to teach procedural writing during a unit on the scientific process; informational expository writing may complement your American history unit. Remember that descriptive writing skills are integral to all genres and should be taught and reviewed in a cyclical manner throughout the year.

Events like story contests, public speaking competitions, and poetry month may be highly motivational for your students. Mark your calendar and be sure to exploit these teachable moments. Make writing instruction meaningful for your students. The end goal of their writing should not be a grade or score. Purpose should always be greater than a score and an audience loftier than an assessor.

Final Words: What Is Good Writing?

When we step back and become reflective about our professional practices, we gain powerful perspective and often create philosophical shifts that shape our approach to teaching. Concerning the teaching of writing, it is important that we ask ourselves *why* we are teaching writing and what we hope to accomplish through our instruction.

Writing, as discussed earlier, is an expressive language process. Working to develop writing skills will reap reciprocal benefits in the related language processes of listening, speaking, and of course, reading. To limit or ignore one of the language processes is inherently detrimental to the rest. As conscientious educators, we must fully address both receptive and expressive language processes to ensure our students' optimum achievement.

Beyond its importance as a spoke in the wheel of language processes, writing is essentially a form of communication. We want our students to become adept at communicating because this will contribute to their success as well-rounded, productive citizens. Therefore, effective communication is a supreme goal of writing instruction.

Written communication occurs between two subjects—the author and the reader. Therefore, writing cannot be taught as a solitary skill brought forth from the transmitter. If effective communication is our goal, we must always exalt the importance of the reader as the intended receiver and help our students understand that effective written communication is that which creates meaning and pleasure for the reader.

So, what is *good* writing? Good writing is good reading. We teach craft skills, conventions, and organizational strategies because they all work together to create meaning and interest for the reader. *That* is the goal of writing instruction.

We know we are successful as educators when we are able to lose ourselves, if only for a moment, in a student's writing. To become absorbed in the images created by the author, to achieve a new perspective, or to mentally meander into the beauty of the way words were artfully chosen and laced together is a diversion we welcome and desire.

The superficial challenge presented to today's teachers is to build young writers who can achieve optimum scores awarded by assessors; however, our true challenge should be to guide students into becoming authors who cause us to forget that we are teachers and remember that we are readers.

Appendix

Personal Description

Write a description of yourself. Think about:

EYES	HAIR	SIZE	SMILE
HOBBIES	TALENTS	PERSONALITY	SKIN

Write descriptively, using interesting color words and comparisons. Use strong verbs and begin sentences in different ways.

Weak example: *I have black hair. I have freckles on my nose. My teeth are shiny and white. I am tall. My smile is friendly and kind. I like to write. I like to sing.*

Strong example: *My long, dark hair is the color of the midnight sky. Small freckles sit on my nose like specks of brown paint. Shiny pearls sparkle when I smile and even though my towering height can be overpowering, people can easily see that I'm friendly and kind. Writing is my passion and singing is my joy. I am an artist with words and sound.*

Now, write to describe yourself:

Character Description Activity

Hair:

Eyes:

Nose:

Lips:

Dress:

Shoes:

Manner:

Use the descriptive words above to write a brief paragraph describing the character:

Setting Poem

Name: ______________________________

Picture your setting.

1. Down the middle of the page, list five nouns that you see in your setting.
2. In front of each noun, write one or two adjectives to describe that noun.
3. After each noun, write a strong verb.
4. After each verb, write an adverb, a prepositional phrase, or a simile where appropriate.
5. Link the lines together so they flow as a poem.

Example:

This began with five nouns: *trees, stones, water, leaves, banks.*

"The Creek at Stone Mountain"

Beneath the sheltering canopy of **trees**
Smooth, glossy **stones** shimmer with fragments of golden sunlight.
Glassy **water** rolls slowly, softly, like a lullaby.
Emerald **leaves** sparkle overhead and long, soft grasses cushion
The deep muddy **banks** of the creek at Stone Mountain.

Interactive Glossary

Alliteration	My example:
Asides to the Reader	My example:
Beginning Techniques	My example:
Clues for Inference	My example:
Descriptive Attributes	My example:

Dialogue	**My example:**
Dialogue Tags	**My example:**
Embedded Definitions	**My example:**
Ending Techniques	**My example:**
Hyperbole	**My example:**

Metaphor	**My example:**
Onomatopoeia	**My example:**
Personification	**My example:**
Repetition	**My example:**
Rhyme	**My example:**

Sentence Variation	**My example:**
Simile	**My example:**
Specificity	**My example:**
Strong Verbs	**My example:**
Transitional Devices	**My example:**

Voice	My example:
Additional Skill: ____________________	My example:
Additional Skill: ____________________	My example:
Additional Skill: ____________________	My example:

On-the-Spot Intervention Guide

While the topic of writing intervention can fill a separate book, there are a few common roadblocks for children and some quick tricks that can often help them move forward in their writing development. If you encounter any of these common roadblocks, try these on-the-spot interventions.

Writing Roadblock	Try This...
The emergent writer with weak fine motor skills has difficulty transferring from dictation to writing.	Some students are cognitively ready to begin writing, but you're still waiting for their fine motor abilities to catch up. Use a yellow highlighter to form the letters the child hears in his or her spelling approximations and allow the child to trace over the highlighter with a pencil. This way, the child can achieve the essential cognitive milestone while still allowing the fine motor skills to develop.
The child has difficulty writing complete sentences.	Some children fill the page with run-on sentences and sentence fragments. It is essential for these children to learn to *listen* to their own writing. If you see this happening, read the piece out loud to the child as written. Ask the child to tell you where sentences should begin and end. When getting started on a new piece, have the child verbalize sentences for you before writing them.
The child consistently misspells high-frequency words in his or her compositions.	Even after acing a spelling test, some children can't seem to transfer this accuracy into their daily writing. Select three words to target at a time. Stick those words to the child's desk, in the writing notebook, and in permanent marker on the child's pencil. Hold the student accountable for spelling those three words until it becomes habit. Then, pick three new words and repeat the process.
The child has difficulty organizing his or her thoughts.	Many children are convergent, rather than divergent, thinkers. It's hard for them to narrow topics and isolate supporting details. Using the child's verbalized ideas, walk him or her through the planning process step by step; construct the graphic organizer with the child. Once the roadmap is drawn, these children can usually follow it independently. Over time, gradually hand the planning process over to the child.
When faced with a blank piece of paper, the child freezes up with anxiety and can't get started.	This problem is a particular nuisance in the world of timed, prompted assessments. Give the child a fallback beginning technique—one that will fit any piece, any genre. If the child always has the first couple of words ready, sometimes that's all it takes. I like to use a *setting* beginning technique: *Picture this* or *Imagine this.* The child describes the scene and launches the writing.
The child writes dialogue (absent of punctuation and dialogue tags) instead of telling the story.	This is a common problem I like to call *converstion-itis: What's that? I don't know. Are you scared? Yes. Me, too.* I ban these children from using dialogue. They must tell what happened without characters speaking. To begin with, I give them suggestions for rewriting what they have: *I heard a loud thud. Ginger heard it, too. Suddenly, we both felt scared.* Once cured, students can gradually re-introduce dialogue into their writing—one or two tagged lines per story.
The child needs to add elaboration to several parts of the piece.	Many children are very direct and need to elaborate by adding supporting details, narrative vignettes, and descriptive details. However, there's not room to insert all that's needed. Mark the spots that are ripe for elaboration, and give the child a sticky note for each marked spot. The notes can be lifted to read what's beneath them but will also stay put until time for publishing.

Reading Integration Activities

Below are some activities that can be used as workstation tasks, homework assignments, or independent work following a reading selection. These literature-based writing activities can be used with any narrative story from your reading series and can be used multiple times with different stories for skill review.

Writing: Descriptive Attributes	**Reading: Character Analysis**
Select a character from the story. Look through the story for any descriptive language the author has used to help the reader picture this character. Write a one-page description of the character using descriptive attributes. Include both character traits and physical features. If the author has not supplied many details to describe this character, add your own descriptive attributes to describe the character as you picture him/her.	
Writing: Descriptive Attributes	**Reading: Setting**
Look through the story for descriptions of the setting(s) in which this story takes place. List words used by the author to describe the setting and create a free-verse descriptive poem about the setting. Illustrate your poem.	
Writing: Friendly Letter	**Reading: Character Analysis**
Select a character from the story and write a friendly letter to that character. Include information from the story and ask the character questions about his/her feelings about the events in the story.	
Writing: Strong Verbs	**Reading: Repeated Reading**
Re-read the story. As you read, make a list of strong verbs you find in the story. Be sure the words you list show action that can be easily pictured by the reader. Select five of the strong verbs on your list and use them to write a one-paragraph description of a new character you have created.	
Writing: Strong Verbs	**Reading: Vocabulary/Visualization**
Fold a piece of paper to make eight boxes. Skim the story for strong verbs. Write a strong verb from the story in each box and draw a picture to represent the action.	

Writing: Clues for Inference	Reading: Making Inferences
Re-read the selection and search for clues embedded in the text that lead the reader to make an inference. Jot down the clues that led to the inference. Next, find a direct statement in the text and rewrite it as clues for inference.	

Writing: Organization	Reading: Story Analysis
Use a storyboard to retell the story's main events. Fold a piece of paper to make four sections. Write a sentence in each section to tell about main events from the beginning, middle, and end of the story. Illustrate each section and be sure to include significant details in your drawing.	

Writing: Beginning Techniques	Reading: Survey/Preview
Preview the stories in your reading book. Look at the beginning of each story and see if you can identify a beginning technique that the author used to grab the reader's attention. Select four stories and copy the beginning sentences. Beneath each beginning sentence, write the story title, author's name, and type of beginning technique modeled.	

Writing: Time and Place Transitions	Reading: Sequence of Events
Skim the story and jot down the time and place transitions you find in the order they are used in the story. Consider how each time or place transition was used to advance the plot and help the reader create a timeline of events.	

As you find that selections in your reading series include a wealth of any particular writing-craft skill, (e.g., similes, personification, hyperboles), you can create an activity similar to the strong verb activity on the previous page—students can jot down and illustrate examples from the text of the selected writing-craft skill.

Nonfiction Reading Integration Activities

Students are required to read nonfiction texts both in reading and in content areas. Because descriptive skills apply to every genre, you can also ask students to locate sensory words, descriptive attributes, strong verbs, etc. in nonfiction selections. Other ways to integrate writing into nonfiction reading are:

Writing: Thesis Statements	**Reading: Main Idea**
Re-read the nonfiction selection and look for main idea sentences. These sentences can usually be found at the beginnings of paragraphs. Fold your paper to create four boxes. In each box, copy a main idea sentence from the text and draw an illustration that includes supporting details from that paragraph.	
Writing: Organization	**Reading: Comprehension**
Re-read the selection. On an expository graphic organizer (concept web, boxed flow chart, etc.), record the main ideas and supporting details found in the selection.	
Writing: Types of Supporting Details	**Reading: Comprehension**
Think about the types of supporting details you have learned. Create three columns on your paper and label each column with a different type of supporting detail (authoritative quote, numbers, narrative vignettes, etc.). Re-read the piece and make a bullet list of supporting details in each column.	
Writing: Comparisons	**Reading: Compare/Contrast**
Draw a Venn diagram or use a CraftPlus Comparison Organizer to compare two central figures in the selection (two different animals, structures, forces, locations).	

Sample Writing Warm-ups: Progressive Skill Practice

Strong Verbs, Day 1:

Write a strong verb alternative for each of the following verbs. Use two of your strong verbs in a sentence.

Went ________	**Looked** ________
Ate ________	**Walked** ________

____

Strong Verbs, Day 2:

Think of your favorite hobby or activity.

1. **Draw a picture that shows you active in your hobby or activity:**

2. **Write five strong verbs that tell about your actions:**

__________ __________ __________ __________ __________

Strong Verbs, Day 3:

Look at the picture you drew and the strong verbs you listed yesterday.

Use the strong verbs to write a description of yourself when you are involved in your favorite hobby or activity (3-4 sentences):

____

____

____

____

Sample Writing Warm-ups: Various Craft Skills

Descriptive Language:

Write two describing words for each of the following **descriptive attributes**:

Size:	____________	____________
Shape:	____________	____________
Sound:	____________	____________
Taste:	____________	____________
Texture:	____________	____________

Simile:

Write a **simile** (using *like* or *as*) in a sentence describing yourself.
(Example: *Once I get warmed up, I can play air hockey like a world-class champion!*)

____

____

____

Metaphor:

Write an object of comparison for each of the following:

Dandelion	________	Snowflake	________
Car	________	Roller coaster	________
Airplane	________	Books	________

Pick one comparison and write a sentence containing a **metaphor**.
(Example: *Roller coasters are freeways of fun, carrying passengers on the road to adventure.*)

Alliteration:

Select a consonant. List ten words beginning with one sound made by your consonant.

________ ________ ________ ________ ________

________ ________ ________ ________ ________

Then, use some of your words to write a sentence containing **alliteration**.
(Example: *Lilting leaves lingered in the air before landing on the ground.*)

____

____

Onomatopoeia:

Create your own **onomatopoeia** by writing a "sound word" for each of the following:

A bouncing ball ____________________

A fast car ____________________

A hungry chicken ____________________

An old door ____________________

The night wind ____________________

Ocean waves ____________________

Dialogue:

Write a line of dialogue for each of the following characters. Be sure to include a dialogue tag and use correct punctuation.

A teacher speaking with the parent of a child who has just won an award:

____

____

A teenager ordering fast food:

____

____

Personification:

Complete the chart to give human actions and qualities to non-human entities. The first one is done for you as an example.

Non-human entity	Action verb	Attitude
Rain	*dancing*	*joyful*
Wind		
Clouds		
Flower		
Car		

Choose one non-human entity and write a sentence using personification:

Example: *The joyful rain danced on the sidewalk.*

____

____

____

Long-range Plan for Writing Instruction

Marking Period: ______ *Genre:* ______________________ *# of weeks:* ________

Craft Skills:	Literature Models:	Practice Activities:	Mini-assessments:
Genre Piece and Theme:	**Planning Strategies:**	**Differentiated Instruction:**	**Assessment:**

Long-range Plan for Writing Instruction (Sample)

Marking Period: 1 ***Genre: Descriptive Writing*** ***# of weeks: 3***

Craft Skills:	**Literature Models:**	**Practice Activities:**	**Mini-assessments:**
Strong verbs	*The Wind Blew by Pat Hutchins*	*-Partners list actions in a picture prompt and compose brief practice piece (2-3 sentences). -Students work independently to list action words in picture prompt and compose brief practice piece.*	*Each student lists five strong verbs associated with a favorite activity (e.g., soccer, tennis, video games) and writes a brief composition (3-4 sentences) including all five verbs. Illustrate.*
Sensory words	*When I Was Young in the Mountains by Cynthia Rylant*	*-Review adjectives and five senses. Read model; students jot down sensory adjectives. Make class chart and continue to add sensory adjectives.*	*Each student writes a descriptive paragraph about a food item and eating establishment (real or created), pretending to be a food critic for a newspaper.*
Beginning technique: onomatopoeia	• *Berlioz the Bear by Jan Brett* • *The Little Engine That Could by Watty Piper* • *Big Al by Andrew Clements*	*-Partners list sound words related to classroom. -Students work independently to write several sample beginning techniques using onomatopoeia.*	*Each student selects one of the practice pieces and adds a beginning technique using onomatopoeia.*
Ending technique: circle back to the hook	• *If You Give a Mouse a Cookie by Laura Numeroff* • *I Loved You Before You Were Born by Anne Bowen* • *Ox-Cart Man by Donald Hall*	*-Students work individually to create endings that circle back to sample beginnings written previously.*	*Each student selects one of the practice pieces and adds a feeling statement as an ending technique.*
Genre Piece and Theme:	**Planning Strategies:**	**Differentiated Instruction:**	**Assessment:**
Students select an area of the school campus (classroom, library, courtyard, cafeteria, etc.) and write a one-page descriptive piece using all of the above craft skills.	*Students observe selected area and list sights, sounds, smells, textures, tastes (if applicable), and action words that apply to the selected area. Draft beginning technique (onomatopoeia) and ending technique (feeling statements).*	*Assist with planning and have student verbalize ideas prior to writing. Shorten piece to one-half page and alternate independent writing with dictation.*	*Weighted checklist: (unedited practice) Complete, 60% Strong verbs, 10% Sensory words, 10% BT – onomatopoeia, 10% ET – feeling statement, 10%*

CraftPlus Single-skill Rubric

Target Skills:	3 Student applies skill competently and creatively.	2 Student applies skill competently.	1 Student attempts to apply skill.	0 Student does not attempt to apply skill.
Target Skill: __________ __________				

Teacher Comments:

____

____

____

____

CraftPlus Multiple-skills Rubric

Target Skills:	3 Student applies skill competently and creatively.	2 Student applies skill competently.	1 Student attempts to apply skill.	0 Student does not attempt to apply skill.
Organizational: ____________ ____________				
Composing: ____________ ____________ ____________				
Conventions: ____________ ____________				

Teacher Comments:

____

____

____

____

Samples of Weighted Checklists

Writing - Weighted Checklist - Four Required Skills

Assignment complete:	(60%)	_____
_______________	(10%)	_____
_______________	(10%)	_____
_______________	(10%)	_____
_______________	(10%)	_____

Final score: __________

Writing - Weighted Checklist - Four Required Skills

Assignment complete:	(60%)	_____
_______________	(5%)	_____
_______________	(5%)	_____
_______________	(5%)	_____
_______________	(5%)	_____
_______________	(5%)	_____
_______________	(5%)	_____
_______________	(5%)	_____
_______________	(5%)	_____

Final score: __________

Descriptive Writing Planner

Setting description:	Time and place transitions:	Similes, personification:	Descriptive words (think about your five senses):	Onomatopoeia:

Expository Organizer: Boxed Flow Chart

Beginning Technique/Topic and Focus:
Topic/Ending Technique:

Expository Organizer: Concept Web

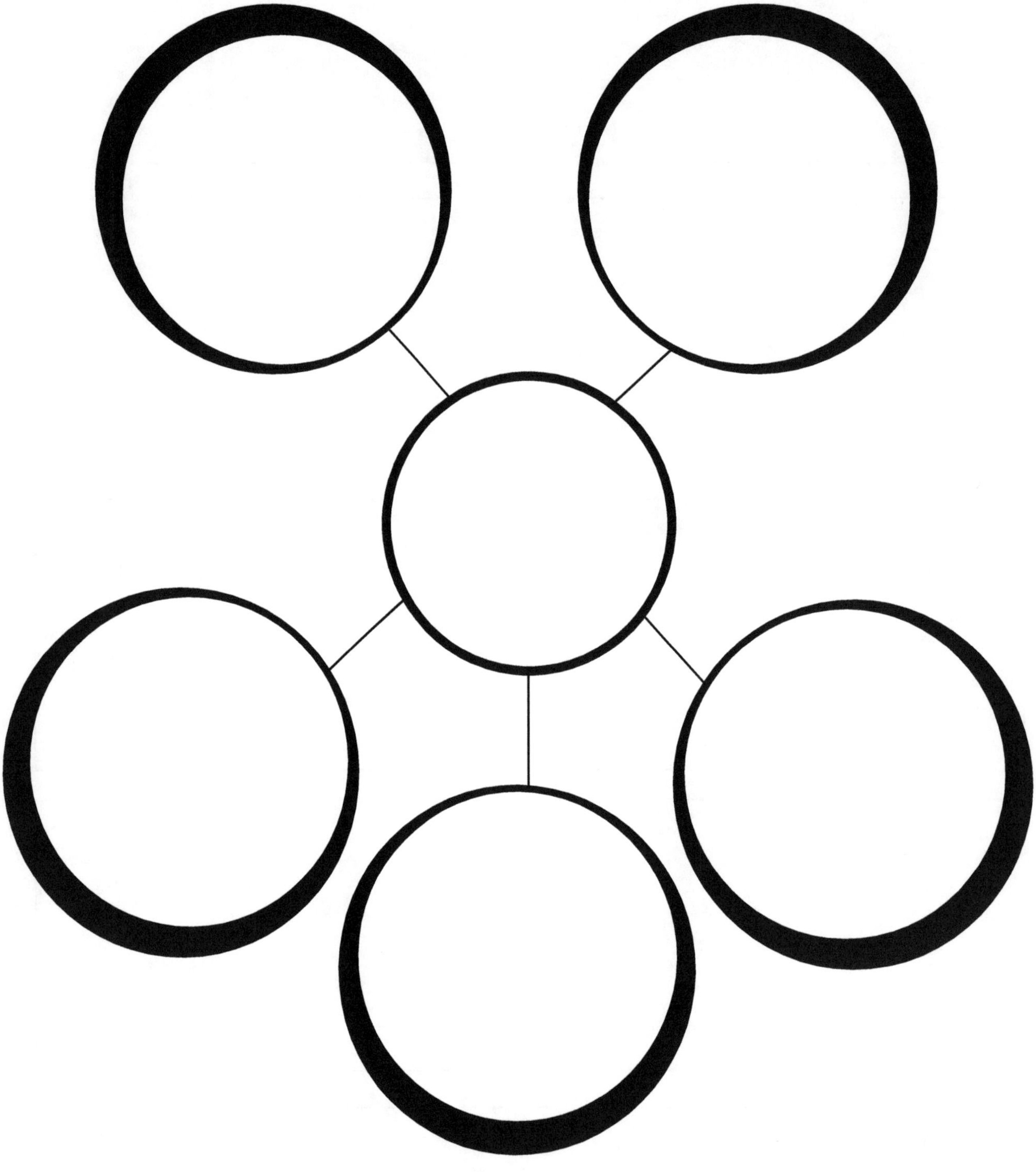

Fictional Narrative Planner

Title:	Character(s):	Setting(s):	Problem:
Event #1:	Event #2:	Event #3:	Conclusion:

Personal Narrative Organizer 1

B: *Introduce main character(s), setting, and situation.

M: *List events in chronological order, leading up to the main event.

E: *Decide how it will end: ___ learned something ___ reflection, looking back ___ feeling ___ character(s) changed ___ something was accomplished

Personal Narrative Organizer 2

B:
M:
E:

Storyboard

1

2

3

4

Primary/Intermediate Revision Worksheet

Author's Name: ______________________________

Title of Piece: ________________________________

Check to be sure you have included each of the following required skills in your piece.

_____ My BEGINNING TECHNIQUE:

_____ At least three TRANSITIONS:

1.

2.

3.

Additional transitions:

_____ I used these STRONG VERBS:

1.

2.

3.

4.

5.

_____ Additional DESCRIPTIVE SKILLS (simile, metaphor, personification, descriptive language):

_____ My ENDING TECHNIQUE:

Beginning Techniques

Onomatopoeia

Ka-ching! Think of all the money you can earn if you start your own business.

Question

If you were asked to pick any vacation spot in the world, what would you choose? I know that I would choose…

Scenario

Imagine sitting in the sterile waiting room of your dentist's office, surrounded by beige wallpaper, bland magazines and plastic plants, when suddenly you realize you forgot to brush your teeth.

Dialogue

"Marcus, have you finished your chores?" As soon as the words came out of her mouth, I knew that, once again, I was going to be in trouble.

Exclamation

Eureka! That was the call of gold miners in the 1800s when they discovered that precious metal in the western mountains.

Mystery/Suspense

It seemed like an ordinary day. The sun rose in its usual way, the alarm went off like it always did, and I rolled out of bed ready for the same old routine. Little did I know, November 13th was going to be anything BUT ordinary!

Common Expository Ending Techniques

Remind the reader

Remember, if you ever find yourself in a house full of germs,
drink lots of fluids, get your rest, and wash, wash, wash your hands.

Give advice

Take it from me, if you want to save yourself a lot of trouble,
just do your chores.

Feelings statement

I just love *writing more than any other subject at school!*

Common Narrative Ending Techniques

Learned a lesson

I learned an important lesson that day. NEVER underestimate your sister's promises.

Accomplished something

It was a tough week, but winning first place at the swim camp competition was worth it!

Looking back

I'll always remember that special gift given to me by my grandmother.

Strong Verbs

Accelerate
Accuse
Aim
Amble
Announce
Bellow
Blast
Blaze
Block
Brush
Burst
Cackle
Cast
Cavort
Chug
Clamp
Climb
Collapse
Collect
Commence
Compete
Comprehend
Crawl
Create
Creep
Cruise
Dash
Devour
Dream
Dunk
Flap
Flee
Flew
Gallop
Gaze
Glance
Glare
Glisten
Gobble
Gossip
Grab
Gulp
Halt
High-step
Hike
Hurry
Imagine
Inform
Inhale
Investigate
Jump
Launch
Leap
Listen
Lob
Meander
Mumble
Munch
Nibble
Organize
Pace
Peek
Ponder
Pop
Prance
Prop
Race
Raise
Release
Retreat
Roll
Scope
Screech
Seize
Serve
Shout
Shovel
Shrivel
Sift
Sizzle
Sketch
Skid
Slam
Slide
Slip
Soar
Sought
Spy
Spike
Spread
Sprint
Stare
Strike
Study
Stuff
Swallow
Swirl
Tackle
Teleport
Throw
Tip-toe
Travel
Trip
Trudge
Tumble
Twirl
Upload
Vacuum
View
Waltz
Wave
Whack
Wince
Zap
Zip
____
____
____
____
____
____
____
____
____
____
____

Types of Supporting Details

Embedded Definitions

Sentence: *Don't fumble! This means don't drop or bobble the ball.*
Commas: *Don't fumble, which means drop or bobble, the ball.*
Dashes: *Don't fumble – meaning drop or bobble – the ball.*
Parentheses: *Don't fumble (drop or bobble) the ball!*

Quote an Authority

In the words of my dentist, "Don't rush when you brush."
Miss Manners, an etiquette camp leader, said "..."
According to our local meteorologist, the weather is about to change.
Mrs. Brinson, a longtime authority on education,...

Numbers

Dates: *On September 21, 1845; Up until the 1900s; By March 2009*
Exact count: *So far, 13,452 people have...; He has won twenty-two races...; Last year there was only one incidence of vandalism...*
Percent: *In a recent survey, eighty-six percent of students agreed that...; My spelling grade rocketed up from fifty-four percent to one-hundred percent after I discovered...; The young slugger is batting .468 so far this season.*
Money: *The event raised 8,300 dollars...; He earns eight dollars per hour; She was just six cents short of being able to purchase...*
Statistics: *Four out of five dentists surveyed agree that...; One in ten teachers will...*
Scores: *Chiles defeated Lincoln 48-45; The Cardinals are up by two games...; The game was a shut-out with a final score of 21-0.*
Time: *At precisely 6:38 p.m.; After about twenty seconds...*

Anecdotes

When my family embarked upon a tour of Civil War battlefields throughout the Southeast...
Believe me, I have learned firsthand the perils of procrastination. Last year, I...
I once had a neighbor who was confined to a wheelchair. I remember a time when...

Comparison/Analysis

My dog longs for human companionship. My cat, on the other hand,...
Sufferers of both type I and type II diabetes share some common characteristics....
If you were able to observe a cross-section of the Earth, let's explore what you would see....

The Four Cs of Peer Conferencing: Compliment, Connect, Critique, and Compliment Craft

Five Ways to Compliment the Author:	Five Ways to Create a Connection:
The beginning was very strong because... *I could really picture...* *You are very good at...* *My favorite part was...* *Your ending was great because...*	*It reminded me of...* *It made me think of...* *I can connect with...* *I can relate to...* *That's just like...*
Five Ways to Create a Critique:	**Five Ways to Compliment Craft:**
I was confused when... *I didn't understand why...* *What happened to...* *In the end, I wondered...* *As a reader, I would have liked...*	• Offer a "Did-it-Dot" each time the skill is used.* • Highlight each example of the craft skill. • Make tally marks on a sticky note each time the skill is read. • Give a "thumbs-up" each time the skill is read. • Jot down three examples of the skill.

*See *Building a Writing Community* by Marcia S. Freeman for more information on Did-it-Dots.

CraftPlus Comparison Organizer

NAME: ____________________

DATE: ____________________

ATTRIBUTE		BOTH	

Bibliography

Bottoms, Laurie. "Notes on the Portfolio Approach to Teaching Writing." *The Quarterly of the National Writing Project and the Center for the Study of Writing* 14.2 (1992): 27-29. Print.

Calkins, Lucy. *The Art of Teaching Writing*. Portsmouth, NH: Heinemann, 1994. Print.

Clay, Marie M. *What Did I Write?*. G.B.: Heinemann, 1975. Print.

Freeman, Marcia S. *Building a Writing Community: a Practical Guide*. Gainesville, FL: Maupin House, 2003. Print.

Graham, S., & Perin, D. (2007). *Writing next: Effective strategies to improve writing of adolescents in middle and high schools – A report to Carnegie Corporation of New York*. Washington, DC: Alliance for Excellent Education. Print.

Graves, Donald H. *A Fresh Look at Writing*. Portsmouth, NH: Heinemann, 1994. Print.

Graves, Donald H. *Writing: Teachers and Children at Work*. Portsmouth, NH: Heinemann, 2003. Print.

Murray, Donald. "Teach Writing as a Process Not Product," *The Leaflet* (Nov. 1972): 11-14. Print.

Piazza, C.L. and Seibert, Carl F., "Development and Validation of a Writing Dispositions Scale for Elementary and Middle School Students." *The Journal of Educational Research* 101.5 (2008): 275-286. Print.

Piazza, C.L. "The More Things Change, the More They Stay the Same: A Survey of High School Students' Writing Experiences." *NCTE: Research in the Teaching of English* 39.3 (2005): 271-304. Print.

Notes: